ONE

SUZANNE
MAYERNICK
AND
GWEN
OATSVALL

IMPOSSIBLE
STARTS HERE →

B&H
PUBLISHING GROUP
NASHVILLE, TENNESSEE

978-1-4336-8408-1

Published by B&H Publishing Group
Nashville, Tennessee

Dewey Decimal Classification: 234.6
Subject Headings: FAITH \ OBEDIENCE \ ADOPTED
CHILDREN

1 2 3 4 5 6 7 8 • 19 18 17 16 15

DEDICATION

In memory of Jan Eberle (1960–2014)—our friend, mentor, prayer warrior, and first official volunteer of 147. Her years of love for us were a priceless gift.

And to all the 147 Million Orphans that we pray for and strive to serve in Jesus' name each day.

CONTENTS

FOREWORD

"HELLO, KATIE?" A WOMAN answered the phone with a sweet southern twang. "My friend and I have been reading your blog and wondered if you'd like to meet with us sometime?"

And so the story began. I knew right away that Gwen, Suzanne, and I would be fast friends when they met me at Starbucks but insisted that we go next door for ice cream instead. That evening was the first of many, many conversations in which we wept of brokenness and then again cried from laughing too hard over heaping paper cups of dripping ice cream full of Heath bar and brownie pieces.

That fall, Gwen and Suzanne adopted me, just like they have so many others, into their families. I ate at their tables, tagged along with them to church and children's sporting events, joined them at the gym, and ate chocolate cake late at night on their couches.

They understood my desire to say "Yes" to God, even when it led me into crazy impossible things. In fact, they shared in that desire and were in the midst of living it out through their own crazy and beautiful lives. They spoke understanding and wisdom over me that few would have been able to. And as one bowl of ice cream turned into more and more, God forged a friendship that went deeper than most can in years.

Years later this friendship is rich with blessings I could not have imagined. Half a world, the Atlantic Ocean, two busy and growing organizations, and *twenty-six* kiddos make communication limited and short. But when we do get a moment to text, talk, or, just a few blessed times a year, sit next to each other, I feel nothing but loved, understood, and deeply thankful.

Just months ago, after having not seen either of them in nearly a year, I sat on Gwen's porch in stitches once again. She was rapidly speaking in sign language to her little boy while telling me the story of the mentally delayed adult their family had just taken in. I laughed, not necessarily because the situation was funny, but because *she got it*. She got it. There we were in her home in suburbia America, and her house was wide open to the stranger, the needy, the disabled, and to me, who was currently more in need of grace and encouragement that any of them. A few days later I flopped down on Suzanne's couch, and her youngest daughter Josie promptly flopped down right on top of me. I nearly cried again, this time with the joy of all that He has redeemed since the first time I met Josie in an orphanage in Uganda in 2006. I marveled, as I almost always do with these two, at the big things God will do with our small, obedient, "Yes."

These two have taught me so much about how to be a mother, and even more about how to be a true and authentic Christ follower. They have taught me to laugh when you feel like crying and to extend the same grace to yourself that you extend to others. They have loved me when I was most unlovable and believed in the impossible with me when the rest of the world thought I was crazy. These two have shown me the love of Jesus again, and again, and again. And the words on these pages—they are not just writing them—they're living them, and it is a beautiful thing to watch.

It is my pleasure to introduce you to two of my very dearest friends, Suzanne and Gwen. May you meet Jesus anew in these pages the way I do each time I am privileged to sit on their sofas or in their over-crowded vans. May you be inspired to find the *One* in front of you today and love hard. Suzanne and Gwen love with their whole lives. Like Jesus. May we do the same.

Katie Davis

Introduction

Impossible Comes Along

IF ANY QUESTION POPS immediately to mind from taking one look at our families, this is probably the first: "How do you possibly do it?" One of us has seven kids; the other, six—and taken together, they are a wild assortment of ages, accents, body types, and skin colors. A living rainbow of impossibilities. So we don't go much of anywhere anymore without being stopped by somebody, asked if all these children are really ours, or at least looked upon with an expression of noticeable surprise—somewhere between charmed amazement and darting eye-contact avoidance.

And that's fine. Go ahead and stare. We saw you. We just know to expect it now, and quit caring a long time ago what other people think of us anyway.

Because, yeah, we realize we're quite a sight, pouring out of our respective vans, taking up a full block of bleachers at Friday night ball games, looking more like a load of Vacation Bible School kids than moms and dads out with their children.

Oh, we could try to pretend we master-planned this whole operation. We could act like we put it together on purpose with careful attention to age-spacing intervals and available bedrooms. We could also try to pretend that we've honed our weekly schedules down to a science, hoping to give the impression that we pull this off every day without breaking a sweat, breaking a nail, or breaking the third promise we made to ourselves this morning not to lose our cool again.

But, no—we're pretty sure we're a dead giveaway.

We know we're not fooling anybody.

So, you're right. If it looks impossible, that's because—on a lot of days—it kinda is. And if we'd known, going in, that it would be like this, perhaps we might've shied away from it and played it a little safer. But we didn't plan all the long-range details from the beginning. Didn't set out to become a melting pot of cultures every night around our supper tables, each person in each chair sharing a last name with us. And, no, we don't play it perfect on any given day. On *any* day, frankly.

But unless we missed a Bible study somewhere, we don't think that knowing all the answers ahead of time or being little Miss Sunshine *all* the time is the required prescription for living out what God expects. Not for us, not for you. Trying never to be caught off guard or never to make a mistake is more than what He asks of mortal beings. He knows us all too well. And so living boldly for Jesus, as impossible as it can seem at times, is really a lot simpler than that. Not easier, but simpler.

Because it's mostly just about loving Him. And loving others. Isn't it? Isn't that what Jesus said? "Love the Lord your God with all your heart, with all your soul, with all your mind, and with all your strength" and "Love your neighbor as yourself. There is no command greater than these" (Mark 12:30–31).

To love God, we admit, can sometimes feel a little airy and mysterious. Hard to nail down. Is it worship? Is it feelings of adoration and spiritual desire? Is it devotion and loyalty and gratitude and obedience? Yes, it's all of that. More and more of that. But to love *others*—this part at least shouldn't really be so hard to figure out.

And yet in doing it—in loving others, in just doing today what's possible—God invites us amazingly into the impossible.

Every day presents us with *people*. They may fly at us from across the den or ignore us from behind their smart-phones. They may appear without warning in our blind spot on the interstate or may show up right on schedule in the middle of an already overcrowded afternoon. They're in our homes, in our workplaces, ahead of us in line at the grocery store, and behind us in the mirror at the place we get our hair cut. People are everywhere—in our presence as well as in our thoughts. By design and by coincidence. Coming toward us, moving away from us. Placed into our lives or dropped into our prayers.

And based on what Scripture tells us, these people basically (as far as each one of us is concerned) are simply there to be loved. By us.

Yes, *loved*. Not dismissed. Not put out of mind. Not numbly accommodated or sent packing down the road as if they're nothing else to us but a guilt trip. Just loved. One on one.

Loving the one who's in front of us.

That's what it's all about.

Personally, that's really the only answer we can give, out-side of God's marvelous providence, for why *our* particular lives look and sound the way they do today. As complicated and challenging as they've been and can often be—yet so ridiculously full of love and heart and laughter and grand adventure—the experiences we've been able to log and enjoy are, more than anything, the natural, anticipated result of this single, baseline principle.

Love One.

And with one glance around the room or the car interior, we get to see every day what can happen when we do.

So can you.

In time, our whole lives can start to spin with perceptible meaning and purpose. Our relationships can move from being fake and forced to genuine and generous. Our gaping weaknesses can become funnels of pure, Holy Ghost strength. Our worst fears can be washed down with huge gulps and glimmers of fresh confidence, gushing from a waterfall of past history, from times when God came through and showed what He alone can do.

With one. Just one.

That's all He's looking for—one who will see the next thing that needs doing, and just do it.

And so this is what we've sat down to talk with you about—not ourselves, not adoption, not orphan care. Those are enormous parts of who we are, obviously, and we'll do a fair amount of our sharing from that context, since it's what we've seen and what we're currently living. But the true star of this show is God Himself, and we pray that His Spirit is the true author behind these words. So based on that premise, our hope is that what you'll gather as we dialogue here with you, between the two of us, will be way bigger than any single avenue of experience with Him.

Now do we want you to hear the plea of the orphans, to recognize God's heart and calling for them? Do we want you to see yourself as part of their ransom, participating in God's eternal, redemptive purposes for the unloved and unwanted? You'd better believe it.

But we are fully convinced that our great God is up to a million things in His people's lives all the time, that He knows us individually and has put us together into His body to function in any number of different roles. We recall, for example, a woman in her late fifties who attended one of our sessions at an adoption conference. She came up to us afterward, told us she really enjoyed what we had to say, but—for obvious reasons—she wasn't in the stage of life to be considering adopting. "But you know what?" she said. "I was thinking as you were talking there—I might go look into something, like, maybe reading to kids after school, the ones who don't have parents waiting for them at home."

Well . . . wow! . . . that's not something we'd said a word about, not in the whole thirty or forty minutes we'd been speaking and fielding questions from the platform. And yet God had whispered a little nugget of specific, instructional encouragement into this dear lady's ear, and had found her open to receive it and act on it.

And we hope, in the few hours you spend with this book, you will be equally as open to whatever God might be showing you and saying to you . . . because this whole idea of *One*—loving one, helping one, serving one, feeding one, being obedient to the next one thing that comes along—can be interpreted into the language of everyone you meet. It meshes with every agenda item on your calendar and applies to every kind of setting you face.

In nearly all your waking hours, something or someone is on your mind or within your up-close field of vision. And the sensitive, surrendered practice of caring for, interacting with, and paying close attention to the opportunities God gives will rarely fail to create something special, both for others and for you—whether you recognize it at the time or not. Because in God's hands, these one-by-one moments fuse together into something we're all dying to know and experience: His will for us.

It's how He brings the "impossible" to life.

In *your* life.

It sure happened like that at our house.

Between the two of us, just over the last several years, we've been—among other places—to China, Honduras, Uganda, and across the United States. We've raised $250,000 from many noble contributors to build the Love + 1 Medical Center in a deeply under-served area of Haiti. We've been part of digging water wells in Sudan and Ethiopia, feeding some of the poorest of the poor in Africa and Central America, while also developing a little fashion line of cool apparel and merchandise that is funding mission and adoption efforts all over the world.

That's at least the thumbnail version of it. We could tell you more. (And we will.)

Then closer to home, we continue to be moms, of course, to these thirteen kids that God has divvied up between our two families. They've now come to include two African-American boys, two Chinese girls, and three other children from Uganda—these last three having been placed on our hearts through our friendship and walking alongside Katie Davis (author of *Kisses from Katie*), who graciously wrote the foreword for this book and has become to us one of God's sweetest, most inspiring blessings. What an unexpected treat when we realized this amazing young woman, whose blog we'd been reading and blubbering through each day, actually lived down the street, and was home from Africa for a few months with her parents. Counting her as part of our families today is as humbling as it is a joy.

And if you think the reason all this stuff originates out of our homes and daily endeavors is because we're super-achievers, one-percenters, do-everything wonder moms, we swear we are just a couple of ordinary housewives. Nothing shouts "global relief ministry leaders" simply to look at us, we promise.

We are not that special, unique, or gifted. We're just not. We are *not* that woman.

And yet, God has kindly (and often uncomfortably) chosen to put us into the action, primarily by employing the same, foundational truth He uses to make *all* His people effective and constructive in the work He's doing—in the world, around the corner, and right here in our homes. We've merely tried to love the one He's placed in front of us, the one He was leading us to seek out at that moment, the one He'd planted in our hearts and promised He'd provide for. And we still keep trying to do it ten, twenty, thirty, however many times a day He says to love *this* one—the one on our lap, the one by our bedside, the ones in need, or in danger, or even a world away but very much at home in our personal prayers.

Love One.

For all its simplicity, this little principle is sure to bump us face-to-face with situations that seem impossible, seem beyond us, seem way over our heads and far past the limits on our capacities. But when we look back later at what God did, giving us what we need for following through on these deliberate acts of conscience and compassion, we begin to see in ourselves a woefully inadequate person who's done (and is doing) some truly impossible things.

How'd you like *One* of those people to be you?

Chapter 1

Ready,
Set, Go

HI, I'M SUZANNE.

And this is Gwen.

This morning, we got thirteen kids up and off to school in under an hour without much of a hitch, so sitting down to start writing a book ought to be a piece of cake, right? Pop a can of Diet Coke, spread out the chips and salsa to heat things up, along with some Cold Stone ice cream to cool it down, park our laps and our laptops by a sunny window, and let the brainstorming begin.

Ought to be easy.

[awkward pause, eyebrows raised at each other, a funny smirk]

Aw, who are we kidding here? We're scared to death. Completely out of our element, intimidated by the sheer size of this, worried that we're never going to find the time or the brain cells to put two thoughts together, much less keep up the endurance to actually finish. We can just *see* ourselves, six months from now, still trying to wad together a bunch of scraps and pieces and rambling stories, no clearer on how to arrange it all than when we first started. Then driving it downtown to the publisher's office at deadline with our hair stringing loose in our faces, panting and out of breath, "Here, is this sorta what you were looking for?"

Uh . . .

So, honestly, we're sitting here today not sure at all we can do this. Not sure we've got it *in* us. Not sure there's a way. Not sure it's even within the realm of possibility—which would be a real problem for us . . . if not for one thing . . .

We feel this way every day.

In fact, we've been feeling this way for years.

And as far as we can tell, it hasn't stopped God yet from doing whatever He wants done in our lives.

At one time—like most people—we thought God's love and compassion for us was our insurance policy against ever being thrown in over our heads. Isn't that the way it's supposed to work? Isn't that part of the benefit package of being a Christian—that we're never supposed to be given more than we can handle? If a life circumstance or a sense of spiritual conviction begins to seriously threaten what we consider ourselves capable of doing, can't we always appeal to God's mercy and opt out on the grounds of His goodness and kindness? If we're His children, if He's our loving Father, then He would surely understand, we think, why we can only go so far into discomfort without it ultimately affecting our happiness. So we wave the white flag, fully expecting Him to pat us on the head and say not to worry about it, perhaps even apologize for maybe asking a little more of us than He should.

Proves how much He loves and cares for us, right?

But here's where our thinking (and theology) routinely get mixed up. When God's Word gives blanket commands to His people, or when it reveals to us the nature of His heart and priorities, or when His Spirit does that thing where He makes our chest burn with spiritual uneasiness for a string of several weeks—long enough until we know it's not just a temporary intolerance to cheese enchiladas—this is not God being mean and demanding. He's not setting aside His love and compassion for us by deciding to introduce us to hard things.

Now would following up on them put us squarely outside of our comfort zone? Yes, probably so.

If we adjusted our brains to think more like He thinks, would it likely require some reconfiguring of what we currently view as normal and necessary? Pretty sure of that.

If we committed to making a radical stretch in the direction of obedience, would we invite some criticism and questioning from people whose opinions have always mattered to us? Yep. Good chance.

But being scared, or making sacrifices, or risking the misunderstanding of family and friends—those are not flaws in God's program or false advertising on the part of your pastor and Sunday school teachers. Quite the opposite. Challenges like these are, surprisingly enough, where the doors to real joy start flying open for you—faster than you can keep up with them—and where your experience of the Father's love reaches more deeply than ever into your heart, down to a depth you'd never really allowed Him access before.

There have been many times, for us, when we've curled up in a ball again on a vinyl hospital chair for the umpteenth time this year, sitting beside one of our sick children, and yet felt the tender mercy of God surround us like a soft, warm-from-the-dryer comforter. We've spent sticky days and nights down near the equator, where a little air conditioning would've gone a long way toward making things more comfortable, yet been completely refreshed by the bright expression on a child's face, eagerly accepting a bowl of food from us as if it was steak dinner. We've seen our homes fill up with twenty, twenty-five kids on a Saturday evening, without having nearly enough cookie dough, Gatorade bottles, and carpet cleaner on hand to deal with the demand, and yet still gone to bed more exhilarated by the fun than exhausted by the fallout.

That's just how God's love works.

It's not for pampering us. It's for taking us to places where we can be part of what He's doing. It's for blowing us away at what our relationship with Him is really supposed to mean . . . and at what it can empower us to do.

Impossible kinds of stuff.

Like writing a 60,000-word book, for example.

But here goes. The impossible starts here.

Follow Along

The motto and mind-set we're calling *One*—loving the one in front of you, focusing on one person at a time, doing the one thing you're called to do today—is certainly not original to this book. It obviously springs from *God's* Book. And so that's where we want to begin ours . . . because in His Book, the simple number "1" is all the math skills you need for seeing Him multiply your life and your joy exponentially every day.

The Bible, we've found, is not just for five minutes of devotional reading over breakfast, or for those last few drowsy moments before bed. More than anything, the Bible is meant to show us who God is—the one who made us, the one who does everything with purposeful intention, the one who cared enough for cold-hearted sinners like us, who reject Him at every turn, to sacrifice His Son for our rescue. Amazing. And humbling.

We forget what a remarkable gift the Bible is. Just think: God wasn't honor bound to give it to us. He could've left us down here with food and water and breathable oxygen, and considered it way more than a fair deal. But that wasn't enough . . . because He wants us to know Him. He wants us to understand the one in whose image we've been created. If His reason for leaving us down here on Earth, waiting for heaven, is so that we can continually, increasingly become more like Christ and bring Him as much glory as our little old lives can muster up, then we need to be as familiar with Him as possible. Don't we?

And in order to do that, God has given us His Word.

So it's hardly a page-a-day calendar thing. It's meant to shape us and change us, to direct us and define us. And though we could live our whole lifetime without even scratching its surface, there's still so much that's right there for us to see . . . if we'll only look. And listen.

Through the words of Scripture, we learn about God's authority. We learn how to honor and worship Him. We learn how we're supposed to treat our families, our neighbors, even people we don't know. We learn how our lives can be molded to reflect God's character.

We learn (as mentioned before) that all His teachings and commandments can be boiled down into a pair of succinct statements about loving God and loving others. That's the way we're supposed to operate. Always. Because that's what His Word says to us as His children.

And that's not all.

The Bible, throughout its many pages, calls us to be generous, unselfish, willing to share. To be disciplined, under control, and in charge of our anger. To be pure, not corrupted by evil. To rejoice, not worry and complain. To tell the truth, not to mislead. To serve, not to be served.

These things are important. And we're meant to make them a part of our life every day. They are principles of truth, sure to bring blessings, and consistent with people who have been set free to serve Him by the much undeserved grace of God.

In fact, it's that very understanding—God's grace being given to undeserving sinners—that reveals one of the main aspects of God's character, and then personalizes it so we can understand it.

Here's what we mean. The Bible says, "Pure and undefiled religion before our God and Father is this: to look after orphans and widows in their distress and to keep oneself unstained by the world" (James 1:27). His heart, in other words, is for the lonely and voiceless, the weak and unnoticed—the person who's hungry and needs something to eat; the one who's thirsty and needs something to drink; the stranger in need of a home; the naked in need of covering; the sick in need of care; the prisoner in need of a friend (see Matt. 25:35–36).

Yet something inside us just naturally bristles at this line of thought. It sounds so messy, so borderline dangerous, so disruptive to our equilibrium and schedule. It'll cost us money. It'll cost us time. It'll make us more tired than we already are (if such a thing is even possible). Besides, it won't affect just us personally, but our whole family. And in the end, if past experience holds true, we'll probably only succeed at getting burned, misused at the hands of people who survive by taking advantage of those who are simply out there trying to help them.

Just doesn't sound like a good idea, does it?

Surely our church has a committee for doing stuff like this.

But that's because we're looking at it all backwards—as though we are better and more deserving of favor than those who make up the "orphans and widows" category of society. No, no. We too were the ones in distress who needed rescue from our desperation and poverty. We were the ones so stained and polluted by our sins and circumstances that we were unworthy, undesirable, unacceptable to a holy God. Yet He chose through Christ to bring us into His home and family anyway, even going so far as to "prepare a place" for us (John 14:2–3), to enter into relationship with us, enabling us to live with Him forever.

That's what makes it a privilege to be His hands and feet in serving those around us. When people are hungry downtown, or all alone without family, or dying of malaria in Africa, He invites us through His Word into this incredible experience of helping others "in their distress"—not because He wants to be overbearing and burdensome toward us, stealing all the fun from our Friday night plans. He simply wants us to experience in real life the kind of joy *He* feels from having pulled us up from the depths of our hopeless suffering, from having counted us, against all odds, as His friends, as His children.

We *get* to do this. We're *meant* to do this.

Where much is given, much is demanded.

Does that make obeying His Word easy to do? No, it doesn't. His reaching out toward us, as you recall, required a cross, blood, torture, agony. Nothing easy about it.

No reason to expect it to be easy on us either.

Except for this—we do it by dealing with just the *one* thing He puts in front of us right now, whether by a verse He quickens to our attention, a person He places within our path, a nudge He gives us by way of His Spirit, or whatever method He chooses, in order to show us how He wants us to obey His biblical calling this afternoon.

Because whatever it is and however He does it, one thing we know for sure: He's leading us by His love into a deeper experience with Him by giving us opportunity to care for others in His precious name.

Excuses, Excuses

(*Suzanne*) So, yeah, when God started working on Mike and me, causing us to consider the idea of adopting—we already had four children who were way more than enough for me to handle. I remember noticing, in fact, how the jump from *three* to *four* children had created the most drastic sense of overload I'd ever experienced as a mom. Not that MillerAnne, our fourth, was such a wretched handful or anything, but—if you're a parent, then you know—sometimes there's just a dynamic that happens, a lightbulb that goes off, where you suddenly realize how significantly outnumbered you are. And for me, I felt it most dramatically when going from three kids to four.

So I was initially very resistant to the whole notion of adoption. If four kids were proving to be beyond my limit, then what could I expect from adding a fifth?

But I just couldn't shake what I was feeling. The more I prayed, and the more I talked, and the more I pondered what God's Word said about the orphans, I started to realize I was coming to that point where, okay—"Are you going to be obedient to what I'm showing you to do . . . or not?"

And no sooner had my husband, Mike, and I landed nervously on that *One* square of obedience than God started pointing to the next one—to see if we meant business.

In some of the reading I was doing, trying to gain exposure to as much available information as I could find, God had been highlighting in my mind some reports about African-American children—how they were typically the last ones, especially boys, to be adopted from here in the States, and how they more commonly lacked a father in their lives, a statistic that was largely fueled by a disparity in the number of black men detained in the prison system.

So while God was beginning to logically lay all this out for me, training my heart in that direction, He'd also led Mike to a book that really tugged on him in this whole area of needing to lean out of our comfort zones. It was at about this time, too, that Mike was on his way to go hunting one Saturday morning, and heard on the radio or something how the Muslim faith was targeting and attracting increasing numbers of black men, capitalizing on the absence of fathers in the African-American community, as well as in the church.

It was *one* thing, building on *another* thing, laying groundwork for the *next* thing, until we looked back and realized without much doubt at all that these individual steps were leading us toward a clear but ground-shifting conclusion.

(Gwen) And for Scott and I, the same pattern as Mike and Suzanne's held true, even if the details were quite a bit different.

Scott was only eleven months old when his dad abandoned him. So pretty much from the beginning of our marriage, Scott was dead-set on having only one child, total. "That way," he said, "I can pour my life into one kid and be the perfect dad—give our child everything I didn't get when I was growing up." When I later became pregnant with Elijah, to go along with our first son, Jeremiah, Scott said, "Okay, two. But that's it." End of discussion.

Well, four adoptions later, I can tell you now—and Scott would readily admit—he was initially an adamant "no" every time. But this book (and our lives) are not about taking four steps, just one. And so with each new opportunity that came along, as I "submissively" prayed for my husband's heart to open, God kept putting the right triggers in his life—one by one, one by one—until Scott finally wadded up his list of objections and said, "You know what? All my reasons, they all have one common theme. They all have something to do with *me*. They're all selfish."

See, I could've told him that (wink, wink).

(Us) So in each of our cases, just in terms of our adoptions, this is how God used that principle of *One* to draw us closer and closer to Him, more in conformity with His Word, directing us toward lives today that—while still far from perfect, very much a work in progress—are rich with Him and rich with love.

Simply by being willing to say yes, we've not only adopted seven children into our families, but we've also spearheaded efforts that have sent (and continue to send) hundreds and hundreds of cans of baby formula to needy families in Haiti. We've installed an electrical generator and stainless steel industrial appliances to a kitchen there, where volunteers were trying to run a feeding program with little more than a couple of cooking pots. We've provided hundreds of thousands of meals in impoverished areas of the world like Uganda, equipped two children's homes with water filtration systems, even outfitted one of them with all new beds and mattresses after their facility was overrun by a bug infestation. As you'll read later, God used us as His hands and feet to rescue an entire village in Honduras from near demise, turning it into a thriving development where the families are healthy, the kids are learning, the people are working, and hope springs anew every morning.

And that's not all. Nor is it the end of what we intend to do as God keeps saying, "Go here," and we keeping saying, "Yes, Lord." People are helped. Children are saved. The hungry are fed. The joy can't be contained.

And that's why we don't have a problem speaking boldly about this, because we know when we talk about being faithful to the next *One* that God gives you, we're actually only challenging you from a standpoint of love and kindness and friendship. We're wanting you to enjoy a measure of purpose and fulfillment that may be missing from your life, the way it was once missing from ours. We're inviting you to see so much more of yourself and your capabilities when you put them a hundred percent into the trustworthy hands of Jesus.

We all, of course, can come up with our excuses for backing away from obedience.

"I don't have enough money."

"We could never afford it."

"I don't have enough time."

"I'm stretched thin enough as it is."

"I was wanting to watch TV tonight."

"That's my day to go to the spa."

"I can't be like those other people."

"They've got a temperament I don't have."

"Our house is too small."

"Our problems are too big."

"My job is too demanding."

"My life is too hard."

We could use up a lot more ink, just rattling off the end-less barrage of objections we fling back at God and His Word, saying, "I understand You mean all of this in theory, Lord, and I realize it's technically important to You that I do this. But You know it would only overwhelm and upset me right now."

Yet that's how our "right now" delay of disobedience becomes a pattern that follows us through every "right now" moment for the rest of our lives. And by the time we're done, we've blown past a million opportunities to know God more intimately and to bring Him an everyday offering of honor, one by one by one. Instead, we've wasted a whole lot of time and squandered a whole lot of joy at our own stupid, selfish expense.

It's just not a good payoff.

So if somebody were to ask you today, "Where do you feel like you've been resisting God? What has He continually been bringing to your attention but you're deliberately choosing to ignore? When was the last time you had a clear opening for being obedient to His Word, to His Spirit, to the prodding of His presence—and you swallowed it down? You knew what you should do, but you decided against it. How come?"

Look, don't think you're alone in feeling convicted by these questions. We're actually sitting here looking across the table at each other right now, and confessing our own sorry reasons for times when we've picked ourselves over our Savior.

But what if the only thing that's keeping you from coming out with a quicker "yes" the next time is a very basic perspective that says, "Well, hey, let's just do this *One*—it's only one—and see what He does with it, see where He takes us"?

Might be someplace incredible. Even someplace you thought was impossible.

But at the very least, it'll put you squarely in His will.

And that's a good, good place to be.

So let's get to know what God, through the Bible, commands His people to do, to be, to care about, and to work toward. Let's be sure, while we're hustling around trying to pack lunches and schedule meetings and grab a workout and make our endless doctor's appointments, that we're giving priority to hearing from God and listening to His Word. Because if God says something is important—for you, for any of us, for *all* of us—then not only should it rise to a level of significance in our lives, but it also means this: it must be possible to do (with His help, of course), or else He wouldn't have told us to do it, no matter how impossible it may seem.

Here's our dare to you, then. Ask God to start piquing your heart with what's on *His* heart. Ask Him to start bringing it to mind in the middle of the day and waking you up with it in the middle of the night . . . if He isn't already. Ask Him to keep it front and center as you pray, causing it to share time and even take precedence over your same old concerns for the same old matters.

What might that thing be? That's not for anybody else to tell you. Though all of us as believers are called by God to conform our hearts to what He loves and values most, some of the specifics for how this plays out in our lives are as individual as His creation of us. Is He calling you to adopt? Maybe yes, maybe no. Is He calling you to serve the widows in your church or on your street? Could be. Could be a *lot* of things.

And sure, whenever His Spirit really begins to birth something in your heart, you can expect a full platoon of excuses to start lining up in self-defense. We're each an old hand at that. Our skill at manufacturing excuses and justifications for our behavior is one of the last things to go, even after we lose the ability to call our children by their right names the first time (or second time, or third time), even when we routinely can't remember where we parked our car thirty minutes ago at Target. But if you decide, finally, to push that big pile of excuses out of the way, irritated by them, you can expect something else to show up that provides a much softer landing spot for your fears: the desire to actually do what God's saying.

When He gives that to you, you know He's positioning you for some God-sized experiences.

And you don't want to be excused from that.

Start

Perhaps, even this few number of pages into the book, we've already lost some people who felt like we were taking them places they didn't want to go. And if so, well . . . we're not surprised. You'll find along the way, despite the fact that we're honestly a big, hot mess of mistakes—two women who continue to give our families plenty of unattractive moments to choose from—we've stopped even trying to keep from just saying what we think. Based on what we've seen and undergone and found to be true in attempting to follow our faithful God, He's given us a new courage for declaring His Word and letting the chips fall where they may.

So in reminding you what the Bible says about things like orphan care, and active compassion, and spiritual service, and grace-based ministry, understand what's happening here. People sometimes say to us, when we talk to them about adoption, "Well, we didn't know. We weren't really aware of the magnitude of this issue. We didn't know the Bible actually said that."

To which we usually say, "Well, now you do."

Or as the writer of Proverbs put it, "If you say, 'But we didn't know about this,' won't He who weighs hearts consider it? Won't He who protects your life know? Won't He repay a person according to his work?" (Prov. 24:12).

There's a reason why the Bible is called a double-edged sword, not a Double Stuf Oreo.

So will you do it? Will you do what His Word tells you to do? Will you do what you've been placed on this earth to fulfill and accomplish? Will you set your heart free from others' protective voices and expectations? Will you realize what's most important about being a wife, a husband, a mom, or a dad, and transform these roles of yours into everything God desires them to be? Whether single or married, with children or without, will you take a brave step in the direction of impossible and let *God* decide if it's too much for you and for everybody else to handle?

If you won't do it, then why not?

Give us one good reason.

We'll go you *One* better.

Chapter Break

So just to give your head a breather, and to help frame up this whole *One* theme with some extra bits of context from our crazy lives—oh, and maybe just to have a little fun, too—we've decided to pull over for a second at the end of each chapter to chill and regroup, make sure we're keeping it personal. For us. For you.

(*Gwen*) Because like we said in the intro, we feel a little outmatched by life every single day. And we're betting you do, too. Just too much to handle, too many catch-me-by-surprises, too many legs waiting to spring loose from this octopus. But then there are *those* days, you know?—the ones that become, like, the granddaddy of *all* days—the ones when everything comes completely off the hinges and makes all the others seem somewhat manageable by comparison. Suzanne, I think, may have one of the best ones . . . remember? Christmas?

(*Suzanne*) Yeah, we were just a few days' short of the kids being out of school for the holidays. And I was running around the house, trying to get everything done. I look up at the clock and—man, there was somewhere I needed to be and should've left, like, ten minutes ago. So I went to grab my two preschoolers, prepare to throw them in the car, when—one of them had dumped baby powder all over the other one, then all over himself. Unbelievable.

But I didn't have—I just—I just didn't have time right then to get them dusted off and changed and halfway presentable. So I scooped them up, ran outside, got into our van, which—okay, Mayernick tradition. We always deck out the inside of the van at Christmastime with tinsel and greenery and flashing Christmas lights. But soon, those weren't the *only* lights flashing in my rearview mirror as I sped along with my two powdered doughnuts strapped into their car seats. We had the *red*, had the *green*—now we had the *blue*.

I wish you could've seen the policeman's face when I spooled down my window, and he prepared to give me the standard icebreaker: "Ma'am, did you know you were speeding?" Instead, the only thing that came out, as his eyes measured the interior of my blinking van, was sort of a blank, perplexed look, as if he was wondering what other kind of domestic or drug charges he might need to bring against me, and whether he should radio for backup.

"Sir," I broke through the dazed silence, "I would love to be able to explain this—why I was speeding, why I'm doing what I'm doing, why my car and my kids look the way they do, but—I don't have a good answer for you today. I'm just tired. And kind of over it."

He nodded. Sort of officially. Sort of . . . well, snickering a little, as I recall.

Because again, life is just a bit too much sometimes, isn't it? More than we can pull off and still appear in full control of our faculties. So in the words of a certain patrolman, I say to you, "Why don't you just go on and have a good day?" And don't worry about what others think.

CHAPTER 2

Fun, Blind Faith

THE TWO OF US met when our boys Jeremiah and Michael were in kindergarten, quite a number of years ago. Pretty soon, we were bumping into each other at ball games, crossing paths at the grocery store, waving from across the room at school events, and just seeming to gravitate into one another's orbits.

As it so happened—or, more accurately, as God so directed it—both of us were in the early stages of our adoption paperwork, each for the first time. So the primary way that we bonded as friends was by sharing our experiences as they unfolded, learning all together about this exciting, exasperating process, as told through the tumble of our individual questions, discoveries, and bouts with impatience. Our conversations, as they began to develop and become more frequent, provided a source of needed camaraderie for us, as well as a safe place for dumping and retrieving all kinds of information.

It was both a hoot and a 1-800 help line, all in the same package.

So as we continued to get better acquainted, we would sometimes spend the occasional afternoon in each other's homes, or maybe watch the other's kids for a few hours so one of us could handle a piece of weekday business or something. Polite chitchat that had simply started between two moms was now becoming more personal, more pointed, more prayerful. We were in one of those seasons of life where we needed somebody to talk to who really understood us, more than even our own *husbands* could always understand us, try as they might. We were full of new concerns, new kinds of appointments to keep, and a new realm of unpredictability that, when expressed to other people, would often receive that look in their eyes that said, "Puh-leeze! Is this woman ever going to shut up?"

In *our* worlds, however, we couldn't talk about this stuff enough. And so we found in each other the sort of sounding board and trading post that provided the ideal outlet each of us needed.

What a blessing.

From where we sit today, here's the only grid we can use to interpret how all of this came together. It wasn't just a girl thing; it was a God thing. What we hadn't realized, back at the time when we each had said our private "yes," surrendering ourselves to God in full obedience, was that He was simultaneously dialing up a friendship for us that would come to fruition at the precise, perfect moment.

And what's more, since we were each following different paths toward the same goal—one adopting domestically, the other internationally—God was exposing us to the distinctions and nuances of both categories, wrapping our heads around a much wider swath of understanding than either of us would've been able to capture alone. By His design, by letting us see the process of adoption from all angles through what was transpiring in each other's lives, He was preparing us for a partnership that would go far beyond mere friends swapping stories around the kitchen table, a passion that would lead us over time to a whole new ministry calling.

So we guess you could say, in our attempt at blind faith, God was opening our eyes to new dimensions of His provision. He was working behind the scenes to give us things that we didn't even know we needed yet, while preparing us for things that we hadn't even envisioned.

And in the years since, we've only seen Him keep it up.

This is one of the great secrets of loving and following Jesus. We say yes to Him from one moment to the next—one-one-one-one-one. And although the upshot of these courageous, loving decisions can at times seem to outweigh us by a few hundred pounds—in terms of what they demand or cost or ask of our faith—He assures us that we can lean back on what we already do know of Him, even amid the unknown, and watch Him make it all be . . . I don't know, kinda fun.

Fun, blind faith.

That's what we've come to call it between ourselves. There's just a dangerous beauty involved in following God one obedient step at a time. There's a thrilling sense of quest and adventure that swirls around situations that would otherwise be boring or lonely or randomly unbearable. When you never know where the next yes—the next *One*—is likely to take you, but you know He'll be filling in the blanks with some version of blessing as you go along, you can just strap in without fear and take off into the grace-based unfamiliar.

Which means, from God's way of looking at it, faith isn't actually as blind as it feels.

And with that said, why not just go out there and have fun with it?

Big Fun and Bigger Fun

Fun—like most of our words—is one that's become almost completely lost in the translation from heaven to earth. Down here, you rarely expect fun to occur without spending more money than you can probably afford, taking time off from work or from your regular grind, carving out a minimum three-day weekend, and participating in some form of activity that your grandmother most likely wouldn't approve of. But even if you clean things up a little, fun is usually at least some kind of escape from reality, a shirking of responsibility—something you sneak off to enjoy with those few precious moments that aren't unavoidably obligated to daily life.

So almost by definition, *fun* is a limited proposition. It's forced to occur within a limited time frame. It's restricted to a limited cluster of happy emotions. And it's most often confined to a limited range of activity choices—basically the ones that are selected by advertisers and screenwriters to exemplify what all the cool people are supposed to find most entertaining. We go have our fun, then we come back down to the real world.

Fun over.

But Christians—which the majority of people classify as not being able to have any fun—actually live with the *opportunity*, at least, to experience more fun than anybody in the world. That's because fun, the way a real-life relationship with the living God is supposed to happen, comes from experiencing the rush of complete confidence and freedom in Jesus Christ. It's a combination of recognizing the access He's given us to His infinite universe of knowledge, power, love, and goodness, teamed up with a willingness on our part to trust that our best life, our most exciting life, our most significant and satisfying life, is most likely to occur in no other place than in partnership with *that*. With Him.

And truly, there's nothing else like it.

It can happen in the middle of an average day, just as easily as it happens on a Sunday afternoon. It can happen without spending a single dime, or buying tickets to a special event, or planning out a leisurely itinerary, or having a bunch of people over to cook out and watch football with.

Most of what we humans call *fun* is cheapened by being time-restrained and temporary. You can feel its energy draining out and slipping away, even while you're right there in the middle of trying to enjoy it. But God's brand of fun is deep, not cheap. Strong, not flimsy. And even when He's challenging you to ramp up toward extreme levels of faith and obedience—the kinds of crossroads you approach by making one, single, "count me in" choice at a time—the feeling on the other side of following Him through the intersection is outright exhilaration.

It's like still having the ocean outside your window, even when you head home from vacation.

Because with Him, the fun never stops.

We're talking about the *real* fun of living in full cooperation with our everlasting Father. Not hiding behind our sins, but letting Him change our resistance into repentance on the fly, turning our lives into a much truer form of freedom. Not bound by our limitations, but watching Him orchestrate connections with other people and possibilities that we could never have known how to put together on our own. Not feeling responsible for how well it all succeeds, yet seeing it snowball into unexpected opportunity anyway—because His will and purpose are so invested in it and behind it.

No, it's not always comfortable, the way a night at the movies can be, the way a three-hour concert with your favorite artist can be, the way a ten-day smorgasbord on a Caribbean cruise can be. But it sure beats that sticky, yucky residue of emptiness and regret, which is about the only thing left over whenever we've decided to settle for self-centeredness and complacency.

That, dear friend, is what's no fun.

And that's what our fun-loving God has been so faithful to show us in the years since He linked the two of us together through the common ages of our kids and the common bond of our next big yes. The closeness and accountability of our friendship, like that of our families, keeps us from caving in to easy-way-outs that might save us a step of discomfort, but would ultimately steal our wonder at what God alone can do through us.

You know, the *fun* part.

Sure, new challenges come along every day—sometimes three or four at a time—enough to keep us on the phone at all hours, complaining to each other about how hard and impossible this life can often be. But with one shot of perspective, God helps us see that even our many problems are actually ironic reminders of His many blessings, and that what He gives us by choosing to work with us is worth far more than what we give up by thinking we can manufacture our own fun by ourselves.

You just can't top a one-on-one—*One by One*—relationship with God for giving you those one-of-a-kind experiences that can last an eternal lifetime.

Here's how we know it to be true . . .

First Time's the Charm

(*Gwen*) After jumping through all the various hoops that had sometimes slowly, sometimes quickly, begun to line up in formation for my husband and me—following our *One* initial leap of trust in God's calling toward adoption—I eventually ended up, along with my friend Carlee, touching down at an airport in China.

Yeah, you heard right.

China.

I'm from Smyrna, Tennessee, okay? Home of Civil War hero Sam Davis, a Nissan automotive plant, and an annual air show that draws a few thousand people into town every spring. *And not much else.* In fact, I grew up in government housing there, helping my parents clean buildings at night, even when I was as young as elementary school age. My biggest dream as a little girl was to someday go to college. "Please, God, let me be able to go to college." But look at me now—soaring high above the Pacific on my way to the Far East, several thousand miles from home and a *million* miles from where I ever dreamed my body and soul would actually be able to take me.

And I couldn't wait. All the emotions. All the work. All the prayer. All the excitement. Much of what was still to come, like everything else in adoption—like everything else in life, really—remained very unknown. Your counselors and agencies do their best to prepare you. And they do it well. But there's no script for how it all plays out. You're told to be on your toes, to be prepared for being flexible, to anticipate the unforeseen, and to keep in mind the big picture whenever the little pictures don't exactly fit into your expectation album the way you'd always imagined.

Yet for every unknown—for every voyage into blind faith—you can be sure that God *always* knows what's happening. As for us, we can't see it all ourselves in real time, which can make for some stressfully "un-fun" moments to go through. But the fun comes from realizing, however it may appear, that He's on top of everything—as well as from looking back years later, seeing it from a clearer vantage point, and recognizing just how on top of everything He truly was . . . and is.

Adopting Emily, actually, turned out perfect. She was a dream. Walking into the room on our first day, where eleven little girls were kept together, I knew immediately which one she was. "That might not be the one," Carlee whispered to me, after I'd motioned in Emily's direction, grinning, barely containing my delirious excitement. "She might've changed how she looks since that picture, Gwen. Don't go getting all attached and everything." But I knew. It was Emily. My mama's heart was already connecting with hers.

While most of the other babies screamed and fussed and wailed after being placed in their new mother's arms, Emily laid there very gently, peacefully smiling and cooing. Within thirty-six hours, she clearly seemed to know—even at nine and a half months old—that I was hers and she was mine. My first daughter. I could see it in her eyes. Still can.

People would jokingly say, after we got back home and they'd had a chance to meet her, after they'd seen how well she was doing and how easily she was adjusting—they'd say, "Hey, let me give you the money for *her*, and you go back over to China and get another one. Because you're obviously good at this."

Uhh . . . no.

Had nothing to do with how good I was. This had everything to do with how good our God is, and that He knew how much I needed my first adoption to go like clockwork . . . because He also knew there were other children that He had chosen to adopt into our family in the future. And none of their journeys home to us would ever prove easy again.

Do you see the beauty in that? In what God was doing? My heart almost wants to break as I recall it, knowing so well who I am, knowing myself the way I do. I'm basically a weak, selfish person. Committed and competitive, yes. But not a front-line soldier looking for the action. And if that first adoption episode had been what it *could* have been—what I'd one day learn from experience it could *actually* be—I might've taxied back into our U.S. airport terminal with my new daughter in tow, then gone home and erased every adoption contact and phone number from every technological device in the house.

Scott had wanted to stop at *one* child, remember? And I could've easily been ready to stop at *this* one, if that's how it would've gone down.

But God wasn't having any of that. In fact, I think He decided to use the relative smoothness of Emily's adoption to go ahead and start doing a *further* work of preparation in my heart—honing my skills in working with *other* adoptive parents, starting right there on the ground, in a Chinese orphanage.

Several of the women and couples on that trip were first-time parents. They hadn't been able to have children, many of them agonizing with infertility for a long period of years. So when people come from that situation, part of the natural mind-set behind this moment when they finally meet their first child for the first time—what's commonly referred to as "Gotcha Day"—is to think of it almost like a party, a big celebration, the grand prize at the end of a long, arduous ordeal. But what some of them don't realize is the fact that what feels to *them* like Christmas, New Year's, and Super Bowl Sunday, all rolled into one, can simultaneously be a traumatic day for the child they're just now getting to see.

Think of it. These children are being removed from the only home they've ever known. They're being placed into the arms of people who don't *look* like them, don't *smell* like them, don't *sound* like them, and don't typically feel *safe* to them, not at first anyway. It may be all happy and hugs and snapshots all around for the beaming new moms and dads eager to post their pictures and memories for folks back home. But the best advice for new adoptive parents in that situation is to go slowly, to be sure they're seeing it from both sides, to tamp down at least some of that pent-up excitement by wisely and discerningly measuring the whole dynamic of the room.

On the other end of the spectrum, complications and delays can always develop within the fluidity of finalizing an international adoption—which can be perplexing for anybody, of course, but most particularly for those who've been on perhaps an eight-year odyssey to get there, filled with all the daydreams and expectations that have led up to what they imagine this Disneyland experience will hopefully be like. In some cases a child can go through some serious attachment issues, and the wake-up call of reality can scare a new parent.

So the ease of Emily's adjustment to me, coupled with the dramas happening all around me, put me in the perfect position for being helpful to some women who really needed a friend in that moment.

Fun? No, not in the traditional sense. Not in the Wally World water park sense. But the depth of gratitude that came to me in watching God at work through my feeble, unqualified heart, speaking life-giving encouragement to others at one of the most pivotal moments of crisis they'd ever faced.

Yes, that's fun to think back on. That's energizing to be a part of. What an incredible sense of awe, knowing good and well that you're so incapable, and yet God still sees something He can use in there—pitiful though it is—for His grand, generational purposes in another family's life.

All because you took *One* step . . . and look where it led you.

Sight to the Blind

(Suzanne) God just knows how to show up, like He did in Gwen's life on that trip to China, like He does in all of our lives—ours *and* yours. He knows how to keep our faith active and pumping. After all these years, He still knows how to give sight to the blind.

And when we're constantly handing Him that *One* next slice of obedience, loving that *One* next person He's placed in our path, the Holy Spirit's way of making His presence known becomes as constant to us as it is confounding.

On any given school day, for instance, another mom might be behind me in the carpool line, slip out, come tap on my window, and ask if she can come have coffee with Gwen and me sometime, because she and her husband are interested in helping fund a project they've seen on our website or heard about through the grapevine. It's not because we know where to fish and generate leads. It's not because we're always out there beating our drum and begging for support. We're way too busy being moms to think of everything we should do to take our organization big-time, even though we're diligent to ensure we've always got the people in place to make our programs and initiatives run with careful, compassionate consistency. And yet God seems to say, "Just give me what you've got, ladies"—blind, deaf, and dumb as it may be—and apparently He finds fun in making sure it's always more than enough.

He was certainly more than enough at *my* first adoption, which—while a world away from Gwen's, occurring here in a southern U.S. state—became every bit as rich for me in numerous, revealing ways. I went into this experience thinking about all the little details that needed to happen, making all the ahead-of-time preparations for how this new baby was going to change our life and routine. But God would soon expand my vision, beyond what I could blindly see through my one single set of lenses, and would give me instead a double blessing that I never really expected.

As Gwen said, there's a lot more happening at the scene of an adoption than just the happy, exciting transfer of one life to a new family. There's also a tragedy. And nowhere is that heartache more on display than up-close with a birth mother who's relinquishing her rights to this child she's been carrying so her baby can stand a better chance at success than she's likely able to give.

It's almost always a situation sparked months before, naturally, shrouded in various levels of guilt and shame, surrounded in many cases by some measure of anger and rejection within her family, and surely by prying looks from others, not to mention uncomfortable changes in her own body. A young girl, surprised to be pregnant, chooses bravely to carry her baby to term. But she deals with it mostly alone, at least not with a husband at home to care for her, not with the baby showers to attend, not with everyone's excited acceptance, not with those tummy-patting encounters with old aunts and great-grandmas. It's not the typical young wife and mother-to-be with the glow of fresh hope on her face. It's not at all what pregnancy is meant to be.

Thankfully, God inspired my friend Brenda to call me—as Mike and I and our daughter Grace were on our way to the location—just to remind me of this very fact. "Remember, Suzanne, during all the excitement you're going to feel, this is also a tragedy. If you don't do anything else, be sure to love that girl the way Jesus would love her."

Those eye-opening words would ring in my ear the whole ten days we were on site—from the first time I met her and through our many interactions going forward. I often found time to talk with her, to pray with her, wanting to make her heart feel whole and be affirmed in the decision she had made. I hoped what she'd see was that if I was genuinely eager to love *her* well, she would know beyond a doubt that I was going to love her little boy well, too.

So some of it was heart-wrenching, yes. Emotional and difficult. But God showed up so powerfully, and was so precious to her. In a special season of life that we *knew* would be a blessing to *us*, He gave us the touching, wonderful experience of being the heart of Jesus to a young girl, captured there at her most vulnerable, her most on edge, her most emotion-ally exposed moment of her life.

And this made Joshua's arrival in our life so much more than even the miracle that each adoption truly is. God, by steering us so faithfully through the blind turns, made it a chance for us to participate in the 360-degree scope of His love. He opened us into the big, wide world of His kingdom, and allowed us to be a part of what He loves doing in people's lives.

Fun, huh?

Just Say Yes

(Us) What we hope you see clearly through these first-hand stories of ours is not so much an insider's look at the adoption process. The biggest life-change we each took away from these extraordinary experiences—more than even the children that God added to our families—was the fact that our relationship with Him just *clicked* in those moments. The Bible *flipped* for us into something it had never really been before.

And it wasn't because we were doing something so huge and heroic. This transformation we're describing—the reason it came about wasn't because we were laying out thousands of dollars and booking round-trip airfare to a whole other part of the world. That wasn't the ticket that changed our whole view on what living with Christ was all about. Those were just the details specific to that particular season of life for us. Perhaps, in your life, it could be something much more intense. Or something less visibly intense, when seen from the outside, but just as intense in terms of the faith risk involved. It all depends on what the Lord has sovereignly selected as giving you the most joy and putting you directly in the epicenter of His will. But no matter what your life is meant to turn up looking like these days, the only thing that a big-fun, faith-filled encounter with Him is waiting on is this . . .

Your *yes*.

Just one little yes.

Maybe you've seen the Reese Witherspoon movie *Sweet Home Alabama*, where she leaves behind her Southern roots to become a New York fashionista and—well, we won't rehash the whole romantic story arc here. But you know, if you've seen it, how lightning strikes the beach when Melanie and her friend Jake are little kids, where they have their first little-boy/little-girl kiss. And then you remember how he ends up, years later, opening a glassworks business, special-izing in these unique creations that form when he places steel rods in the sand, which attract lightning to them, and trans-form ordinary beach sand into these unbelievably cool glass shapes. Not sure about the science of all that, but if you'll just suspend logic for half a second here and try to channel your inner chick-flick escapism, you'll see how one force of action triggered a natural *reaction*, with beautifully amazing results.

And somehow, by God's chosen plan, our surrender to Him—our submission to Him—becomes that lightning-like connecting point where blind faith blinks its eyes and sees the wonders of life with God explode in all its color and splendor.

But those words—to *surrender*, to *submit*—are such nasty words in our normal vocabulary. Our first impulse is to resist them, beauty or no beauty. We may not mind *saying* them too much, but we're not so keen on actually living them.

Surrender.

Submission.

Wrong answer.

We like to see ourselves as being self-sufficient. We like to think we know what's best for us. We like to believe nobody understands us as well as *we* do or knows what we need for making us happy. And so that's just how we prefer to handle things. If we dream it, we can be it. If we want it, we can go after it.

No surrender necessary.

One major problem with this idea, however. We could dream, for example, that we'd like to be Erin Andrews, on point and in person at every big sporting event of the year, standing there on the sidelines in our beautiful blonde hair and our shapely figure, interviewing star athletes and smiling for the camera. Not much chance, though, of that gig being in our future. So whatever's going to come together to make us feel confident and complete in life, it's probably going to need to happen on days when we're not being a thirty-year-old, TV-star, glamour girl. Fair enough?

Yet the door to that level of excitement—and beyond it, actually—is wide open to *anyone* who will simply submit and surrender to God's perfect plan for their lives, as revealed in those inconspicuous little moments that hold your next big chance to say your next personal yes to Him.

Will you do it?

Are you willing to fly that blind?

Surrendered? Submitted? Just surprise me?

We've sure seen this bold and beautiful trait in our sweet friend Katie Davis, who we mentioned to you several pages ago in the introduction. We were so blessed to be some of the first ones privileged to serve her in the work she's doing among children in Uganda. Her initiative and compassion as an eighteen-year-old girl led her not only to spearhead educational opportunities for hundreds of impoverished kids in that area, but actually to adopt thirteen of them as her own, offering them an abundance of love, a home, and a sense of belonging, despite how young she is.

The three of us, upon meeting, just developed an instant sisterhood. As mothers of big families ourselves, we were able to mentor her in some of the challenges of being a mom, even though her own parenting occurs in such an unusual, untraditional setting. But her mentoring of us, showing us what it means to love and serve like Jesus—we'd say it far outranks whatever amount of counsel we were able to give her in return.

Katie truly showed us—and still shows us today—how to live a blind walk of faith.

We'll never forget the time she was over at one of our houses, and her phone rang—a call from a friend in Uganda with an urgent message. At that point, we were managing most all of her work stateside for her. And literally, that very week, we had wrapped up six full months of effort, succeeding in getting all 150 kids (at the time) sponsored for school and for all the rest of the help her program offered to them and their families.

Finally. Done.

And then comes this phone call.

Thirty-six kids, the person said, had been abandoned when the director of the orphanage, for whatever reason, had just disappeared, locking the gate behind him and locking the children inside, uncared for. No one knew right away exactly what had happened to cause this, but—didn't matter—all these children had been left all alone.

Katie, in her gentle, levelheaded manner, simply said, "All right, go pick up a truck, take them to my house, give them a bath and some clean clothes, and take them to church the next day. Propose to the church that if any families can take them in, we'll provide what's needed for their school, their food, their housing costs—you know, everything." And hung up.

Like it was nothing.

"Katie," we said, our eyes sort of squinting at her, "you know it's been all we can do to find supporters for the kids you already have. And we've just now finished doing it, after all these months. How are we supposed to get what you need for forty more? Like, now? We know you're just trying to help. We know what you're thinking. We get what you're doing. But are you sure it's really a responsible move to make? You've got to think about more than just the immediate. A lot more's involved here."

She looked back at us, without a flinch, and then calmly said—as if no other alternative made any rational sense to her—"What if a little child came and knocked on your front door, hungry and thirsty and needing a place to stay? Would you just shut the door in her face and tell her to go away?"

[speechless silence]

Then came the trickle of some dislodged tears from our eyes, watching blind faith in action, knocking us off our feet.

Okay, Katie. Okay.

But still, if part of our job was to be the voice of maturity and adulthood in this situation, how could we stand there and tell her that what she'd done was the wisest thing to do? How could she overbook her support and infrastructure by that much and still expect to stay functional in what she was promising those kids she would do for them?

It was impossible, all right. *Impossible.*

And yet, in the face of such an insurmountable decision, we saw Katie just say . . .

"Yes."

Yes to Jesus. Yes to love.

Yes to an abandoned bunch of helpless children.

Yes to an outlook that was nothing but a blind balance sheet of zeroes.

But that's how faith goes from being a *One* thing to an indescribable thing.

And isn't that a much more fun, adventurous, exciting way to live?

Faith Building

Here we sit at our little writing place today, and we just can't believe what all has developed from the fun, blind faith of those first forays of ours into adoption. Or from the inspiration we drew down from witnessing Katie's unquestioning decision to "Love One" at a ridiculous cost. Or from the various water wells and feeding programs and medical initiatives that have sprouted up from such small starts of faith in our lives with so little vision to work with.

But what can we say? We're just two blind mice, crazy enough to believe that when God said to "cast your bread upon the waters" and "you will find it after many days" (Eccles. 11:1 NKJV), He was making us a promise, not just flippantly building our hopes up. So one by one, by the next one and the next one, we've kept slinging those little scraps of bread out there, sprinkled with a little mustard seed, wherever the ocean of His will desires to take them. And ever since, they've been rolling back in toward the little mouse hole we sent them out from, arriving guaranteed, pretty please, with a whole lot of fun and cheese on top.

If life has not exactly felt too interesting or purposeful lately, if you've been afraid to step out beyond where you can see your feet are taking you, don't worry about what's out there in the darkness. That's God's business to wear the night goggles, to see everything as if it were the middle of the day. Our business—your business, as a trusting believer in Christ—is just to seek out or respond to the next *One* you feel Him calling you toward today. As you do, you'll keep on building up your confidence, based on His trustworthy track record, so that even when you see a blind patch coming up, you can learn to say yes to it in your sleep.

We promise you.

Faith is not sight yet for any of us. We'll all need to wait till heaven for that. But God has brought His promises down to earth for us, so that if we really want to experience the good life, we can cross the next bridge to it on the back of His flawless reputation.

One fun is *some* fun.

Let's go have it.

Chapter Break

(Suzanne) When we think back to the early days of our friendship, so many fun memories come to mind. And then there are the terrifying ones that *ended up* being funny, but not so much at the time.

We were over at my house, working on something related to the new ministry we were trying to get rolling. And we were just finishing up, when before we knew it, something else was rolling as well.

(Gwen) My car. Rolling down Suzanne's driveway. With nobody in it that I could immediately see. So I tore off, hurtling through the yard, sprinting toward the ghost-driven car. Our little Emily and MillerAnne were standing where I could see them, a safe distance away, eyes as big as saucers. But Maggie, my little one? I didn't see her. Was she in there?

When I finally reached the car, which was still just slowly drifting, yet picking up speed, I finally spotted Maggie inside, afraid to budge. I'm banging on the window, "Let me in! Let me in! Unlock the door! Unlock the door!" But all I could do, while she was shaking her head, was to hang on to the handle and dig my feet into the ground as the car lumbered off the driveway and eventually settled into a level spot in the yard.

Whew!

Everybody was safe. Thank God. And we both learned our lesson—don't ever leave your car unlocked, even at home, even for a second. But we also learned something else: Even when you're doing your best and trying to give your life away for Jesus, the unexpected can still happen. No one's ever exempt from making every day a new opportunity to be prayerful and be thankful. We'll always be tempted to look up at the heavens and say, "Really, God? Can it not be any simpler than this?"

But it's all part of faith.

And ultimately, it's all part of the fun.

Chapter 3

Seriously? Me?

THANK GOODNESS YOU'RE NOT here today.

To see this.

Because as we often say to people, "If you ever want to stop by to visit, you're welcome to come anytime. If the car's in the driveway, just drop in. No need to even call first. We mean it. But if you want to come by *AND* you expect the house to be clean . . . you'll need to give at least two weeks' notice."

Minimum.

Or trust us, you might find us in our PJs, hanging out with our kids.

That's just the way it is. On any given day, in any random order, you might find in either one of our homes a wide variety of both structured and unstructured chaos. Like maybe some cookie sprinkles on the floor or the countertop from a fun baking project. A pile of clean but unsorted, unfolded laundry, in and around the area of the clothes dryer. Toilets that may or may not have been flushed the last time they were used, depending on which kid was in there last.

On some days, of course—on more unusual days—the two of us might be getting off an airplane in some city after flying there to speak. Checking into a hotel for the night. Showing up the next morning, appearing somewhat bright and rested because we actually slept eight full hours the night before—no kids waking us up at 2:30 to tell us they spilled some water in the bathroom, in case we wanted to know. We hop up on stage in our cute little boots, sporting our signature "1-4-7" shirts, eager to tell our individual stories, which could sound as if they've got all the makings of a really good, highly entertaining television series.

Aren't we something.

But lest we give the wrong idea, we're always intentional to remind people: "This is not us, okay?" motioning our hands up and down, from shoulder to waist. "What you see standing in front of you today—the look, the vibe, the energy level—this took some real effort to pull off. We're sort of a figment of your (and our) imagination up here. Because when we get back home, we guarantee you—the shoes go back in the closet, the outfits go into the hamper, the volumes of our voices likely go up, and these smiles on our faces go upside down."

Let's just be real here.

"Having it together" is not where we actually live.

The image that comes across in the nicely posed, carefully selected pictures from our blog header—every single one of those are all good-day snapshots, all right? With nice lighting. With everything brushed and dusted off and checked twice again in the mirror. They give only a tiny, tiny glimpse into our lives—not the part with the messy ponytail hair, our take-charge voices, or pizza night the second night in a row. And we know, whenever we look at whatever other people decide to post on their own social media as well, we're only seeing as much of themselves as they want us to see too. We get it.

Because no matter who we're talking about, the reality behind the door isn't always the same as the well-placed welcome mat out front. Good chance there's some hard, unhappy, unflattering things happening back there—if not frequently, at least from time to time. And while we're not apologizing for at least trying to look our best in public, we don't want to be a party to any of Satan's inferiority schemes. There's no reason for any of us to feel depressingly less-than, based on others' best-foot-forward impressions, the ones they want everybody to believe and then feel artificially required to measure up to.

The real them, the real you—and, yes, the real us—are the people we'd all get to see if we were over at your house on Wednesday around 4:00 in the afternoon, or peering over your shoulder into an open ice cream container, or watching you referee a shouting match that spilled over from a kickball game into your kitchen, just as two boiling pots and the oven timer were all squealing, all at once.

Aren't we right about that?

So wouldn't it be nice—less condemning and competitive—if we could just dismiss with all the pride and pretense, and settle into each other's lives with enough honesty and transparency to say, "You know what? Half the time or more, I don't get it right."

As far as the two of us go, at least—we're just willing to admit, today wouldn't be the first day we've ever screamed at our kids. We've gotten crossways with our husbands on numerous occasions and vented a weeks' worth of frustration in five minutes or less. (Or *more*, if they cared to hear it.) We've spun ourselves around at the bottom of the stairs and hollered up at somebody we heard sassing in the background, telling them, "There's no more grace left for you today!"— only to wonder, as soon as the words escaped our lips, how we'd like it if Jesus ever said the same thing to us.

No, we're not proud of all this, obviously. We try. We do. Some days are better than others. And thankfully, the noise in our house is generally more happy and fun than heavy and jaw-dropping, for the most part. But we still mess up a lot. *A lot.*

Because that's who we are.

And most likely, that's who you are, too.

So what's the Lord to do with us—with this bundle of nerves, hormones, and temporary insanity? How is He supposed to accommodate this level of inconsistency, the temperamental streaks, the occasional glaring lack of any semblance of self-control? Why would He ever see fit to trust us with doing the impossible, when we so rarely succeed at managing the manageable for more than a few days' straight . . . on a *good* week?

How? Why? What for?

The answer, we believe, lies somewhere between what we see in ourselves (with horror) and what He sees in us . . .

With hope.

Excuse Me?

(Gwen) I knew me. I had been through two years of . . . just wait, when you get to chapter 5, you'll see what I mean. Impossible situations. Way more intense and fatiguing than anything I'd ever experienced in all my life. By a multiple of maybe a million. I can laugh some about it now, but the skin under my eyes had developed these really dark, really deep circles—not from bad mascara or anything, but just from no sleep, from a scarcity of good nutrition, from a lack of available time or access to almost any form of regular exercise. I'd begun to look sort of like the crypt keeper from old TV and the movies. Maybe a *lot* like that.

Rough.

But we had decided, Scott and I—in answer to another *One* of those nudges from the Lord—to open our hearts and home to two children that we were soon to be adopting from Uganda. A boy and a girl. Based on what we'd recently been through, however, we were quite adamant this time not to check the special-needs box on our application. In fact, if we could've "blanked in" the blank square, the way you'd "*black* it in" to signify your preference and declare what you want, we would've whipped out our "blank"-colored pen and filled in the empty space from corner to corner, side to side. Hard. In all its bright blank blankness. Made sure there was no mistake about this.

When the call came in, however—while I was, oddly enough, sitting with my daughter in her hospital room after a sixth or seventh surgery (I think I'd lost count)—they said, "We have a match for you, Gwen. I know you and Scott didn't check the special-needs box on your form, but the boy who's available—Joseph—is one of only two in his age group that are left in the orphanage. He does have some hearing problems, I need to tell you, but they shouldn't be too severe. Hearing aids will likely take care of it."

Oh, great. Really? Deafness? Seriously?

No, ma'am, that's not what I signed up for.

And to show you what my heart was like at the time—to show you what a mess of selfishness could still gush up so easily from the inside—I thought to myself, *No way am I biting that off. Scott will be my out on this. He was a tough sell in the first place anyway, so this ought to be a slam dunk. I'll go home, tell him the kid's got a hearing issue, blah-blah-blah, no-can-do. And my man will back me up all the way. Consider it done.*

"Well . . ." he said, in a very point-blank manner after I'd posed the problem to him later that evening. "We can't just *leave* him there."

"What?"

"We can't just leave him there," he repeated—only this time, I swear it almost sounded like Jesus' voice saying it, too.

I just stood there, stunned, while he said, "I think we probably just ought to go get Joseph, by himself, see what's up with him, see what he needs, then we'll take it from there."

Isn't that funny? That he would say that? After even *my* yes had become a no?

But there you go. My husband. What a guy.

And what a way to expose the "me" who was exerting its own will into God's situation, who had decided I could just arch my back and stand my ground and fight for myself against His impossibilities, a scenario that immediately clashed with me like plaids and stripes in my pursuit of what I wanted.

Am I being transparent enough for you here? I hope so.

Because that's surely what God was seeing in me, too. But instead of kicking me to the curb and moving on to somebody else that He could more easily deal with, He apparently decided to roll up His sleeves and do the hard work of changing *me* . . . and to show me the impossibilities He could accomplish while He was doing it.

When we got over to Africa, we quickly suspected that the issues with Joseph's hearing were not just hearing-aid deep. He was three years old and had no verbal skills. None. And after getting him home, taking him to speech therapy for a year, sending him to sign language camp for the summer, taking him to specialists and neurologists to try digging down to the source of his issues and their potential solutions, nothing was working.

My "me" wasn't happy.

Know why? Because the OCD part of my nature (which, frankly, takes up *most* of it) wanted to be able to figure this out, figure out this puzzle—to know what to do and know how to do it . . . for Joseph. And you know it, I couldn't seem to pull it off. I wasn't going to be able to heal it by just investigating and agreeing to a simple surgical procedure. The answer would need to involve more than a workable game plan involving professionals I'd assembled who were trained for this kind of stuff.

Nope, if Joseph was ever going to battle through and overcome his hearing issues, if he was ever going to be able to function in school and society and on out into his life, then I myself—the whole sniveling mess of me—would need to immerse my whole self into it. I would need to be more for him than I saw myself capable of becoming. And I would need to be content with a process that wasn't always predictable or often very pretty.

Lord, You know I'll do anything I need to do for him. You know that. But what? And how? It's just "me" we're talking about here.

But, man, what He has done with us as a result.

I'll admit, I still don't always relish taking four classes of sign language a week. Yes, me. In class. There are a lot of other things I could be doing during that time, from the need-to-dos to just the want-to-dos. And sometimes, right to this day, my inner chooser often dreads interrupting my afternoon (again) to get in the car and go over there.

But when the lady at our very first class session stood up and said, "Did you realize that eight out of ten parents of deaf children never learn how to sign and communicate with their own kids?" I said to myself, *Okay, that does it. That's not going to be me.*

I hope you're as shocked by that statistic as I was . . . and still am. Eight out of ten. Unwilling to learn how to communicate well with their son or daughter. Hard to believe, isn't it? But true. Parents will bring their deaf child to the communications center, have them sit down with the interpreter, and let this third-party counselor help them all talk with each other as a family, hashing out whatever's going on between them.

Not me. Not this girl. *I* want to be the one who's able to answer his questions, hear about his day, and tell him stories of Jesus. *I'll* be the one who learns to talk with my son. Our whole family will become adept enough at signing so they can speak and respond in real time with their little brother. Our whole house will be labeled with the hand signs for "computer" and "door" and "window" and "refrigerator" and whatever else we all need to learn so that we and Joseph are fully engaged with each other in our shared life and in our everyday.

And you should see him now. I can't believe this kid who started out with, like, ten words he knew at five years old—"Mom," "Dad," "move," "stop," nothing but the simple basics like that—has now blossomed into a second grader who's reading, learning fractions, his whole world opening up to him through the exploding combination of new words, new terms, new concepts, new triggers, new learning and understanding. The works. With support and encouragement from some excellent interpreters and schoolteachers, he's becoming less and less hindered by his lack of hearing, and more and more empowered to handle any environment he faces in life, doing it with honest confidence . . . and usually at high volume.

Yet with all the work that God has rung up in Joseph's progress and development—causing something new to spark inside him each day, it seems—I know that some of God's most challenging work has been figuring out, not what to do with him, but what to do with me. With *my* issues. With *my* weaknesses. With *my* problems. With *my* frustrating resistance to discipline and effort and unknowns and hard work.

But He just keeps on doing it all anyway . . . because He's not surprised by what a mess I am, or by what a mess any of us are. He's not deterred by His children's constant failures to get it right the first time. He doesn't run out of ways to bring about growth within us, even when it does sometimes require a painful, bone-on-bone kind of process in order to do it. Yet He doesn't give up. He doesn't quit tinkering. And even after we've held up pretty well and walked fairly steady for a period of time, only to slip back at a weak moment into some of our old habits, He still doesn't berate us for our stupidity, but just faithfully steers us back out onto the main road. Back into the traffic flow and pattern of His blessing.

Instead of working *around* us, He chooses to work *through* us.

To help us do what we can't.

Building Blocks

(Us) People look at us sometimes and, without really knowing us, they say, "Oh, I could never do what you ladies do. All those kids. All that chaos. All the traveling and stuff."

Why do people say that? Why do any of us ever feel this way about each other? Why do we jump so quickly to personalize our differences and compare our lives like that? Then we either feel *superior* toward others because we're so enamored with ourselves, or (much more likely) we feel *inferior* to them because we know our faults so well and we don't think we measure up . . . in looks, in achievements, in confidence, in character, in anything.

But for our part—just Suzanne and Gwen talking here—we say it's high time we quit seeing ourselves through the lens of other people's lives. None of us should be wanting or aspiring to another person's journey or story, when we've got a journey and story of our own to be living out and experiencing. Instead, let's recognize that each of us is flawed in many, many ways (us, you, them, everybody), so that, yes, you're right—you really *can't* do a lot of things other people do. But you *can* do what God has called *you* to do . . . because *He* can do it. Because *He* can do the impossible.

When God called the two of us to say yes to some challenges that went far beyond our skill sets and resilience, we felt like Nehemiah, way off there in ancient Persia, basically without a clue, totally dependent on prayer for knowing anything about what He wanted us to do and how we were supposed to do it. It was a daunting, scary proposition, no lie. But in the end, like Nehemiah, the bottom line of trust and obedience entailed just going where God had told us to go and starting to put our bricks down, one at a time, expecting Him to eventually turn it into the structure He desired.

Other people, as God worked in their lives as well, also came and put their own bricks of surrender down alongside us. A birth mother in the South, another out West—they each put *their* brick down in hopes of the impossible. Families we never met, Chinese women who could've so easily aborted their babies with the full blessing and assistance of the reigning government—they each put their brick down, too, doing their part.

Nehemiah, you may remember, summoned others to come participate in the undertaking. "Would you come and help me," he said, "just by building and guarding the portion of the wall that runs by the front of your house? Just *your* part?" Some said yes; some said no. Some did less; some did more. But everyone who agreed to serve, they each brought their imperfect skills to the task, and each of them played a vital role in erecting something that no two or three people could ever have done alone.

So the folks who help us provide medicine and drinking water and life skills to impoverished individuals in some of the neediest places in the world—they're putting some bricks down. The ones who give and support and supply and underwrite the programs we get behind—they're putting some bricks down. We're not all the same; we're not each given the same instructions. And we're not here to compare scorecards to see who's running ahead of the other. But together, as highly unreliable people, yet people who are seeking to align our hearts with God's Word and His promises, we keep saying another yes and keep pulling out our next brick. Putting it down.

Building the impossible.

All of us. All the time.

And so we'd say to you today—however disqualified you may deem yourself—step in here and surrender to God, not because you're expected to be so worthy in your own right, but just because you're invited to be included in what God is building all around you. No need to hide anymore behind walls of shame and incompetence. And definitely not to keep polishing up your walls of public image. Let God start employing you instead to help construct the kind of walls that protect others from danger and provide blessing in His name—the kind He loves to build with ratty old people like us who've quit pretending we're "all that," but who dare to proclaim ourselves "all in."

Bring your brick. And put it down.

Just come be yourself.

Let's Just Be Real

(Suzanne) Being ourselves—it's just the best way to be. Obviously, we're all in the process of learning, growing, stumbling, recovering, failing, repenting, trusting, and changing. But in trying to figure out how to go deeper with God and more fully into His plan for our lives, some of the best advice is the same, simple idea we all gave to our kindergartners when they first started to tremble with those early fears and questions of theirs:

Just be yourself, honey.

Just be yourself.

That's exactly what one of our pastors told me, in fact, after we'd been attending and serving and worshipping at this church for quite a number of months, only to continue being treated with polite but noticeable distance by most of the other members.

Might help, I guess, if I gave you a little background.

We had made the decision, after adopting Joshua, to relocate to another church, one that was decidedly more racially diverse. We wanted him—and later, our second African-American baby, Caleb—to grow up with strong role models from their own heritage and background, while also stretching the rest of us into being part of a fellowship where we could blend in and learn, where we wouldn't just be the all-white family in the all-white church with the adopted little black boys. You know?

But to be honest, it wasn't exactly working out the way I thought it would.

I'm the type of person, when I take on a new project or endeavor, I like to immerse myself in it and learn everything I can learn about it. I want to read all kinds of books, talk with all kinds of people, ask all kinds of questions, and grow completely versed in the whole subject area. Completely soak up the experience, both as an eager student as well as someone who can later teach and help others understand it better themselves. So I envisioned, once we'd planted ourselves in this African-American church, that I'd soon be connecting with some black moms and girlfriends, discovering the inner feel of their culture, and finding out the interesting differences between us—things that don't become readily obvious without truly getting to know people. Plus, I wanted to be sure I wasn't overlooking some important insights that would help me be the best mother to Joshua and Caleb that I could possibly be, even down to their skin care and other such basics.

And yet, for some reason, I wasn't breaking through to these ladies. They actually didn't seem too interested in us, or in me, almost to the point of not approving of us and our family. Or at least that's how it felt. I couldn't figure it out.

This was becoming *impossible*.

But one day during this time, Caleb—no more than five or six weeks old—nearly died right here at our house. Just completely quit breathing, just like that. Thankfully, I had taken a CPR class—still had the pamphlet taped onto the inside door of my kitchen cabinets. So Mike and I instantly laid him out on our island there in the middle of the room and tried stimulating his little chest until he came back around.

Whew! Talk about terrifying.

Turns out, he'd come down with something called RSV (respiratory syncytial virus), an illness that can inflame the small airways in the lungs of young children, especially infants, and trigger the kind of heart-stopping episode we'd just experienced. So as a precaution, after our initial 911 call and the rush to the emergency room, the doctor admitted him into the hospital, a stay that lingered into almost a week.

While I was there, three of our pastors—all black men— came to visit us. It was cordial, of course. We appreciated their concern so much. But I could tell: something about seeing me sitting there in that rocking chair, loving on my little boy, who was all strung up with IVs and oxygen tubes and everything—it subtly unsettled them. I could tell they were paying unusual attention to that.

Caleb, unlike Joshua, came directly from the womb with extremely dark skin, almost Sudanese in complexion. So the color of his little face, legs, hands, and arms, when seen in contrast with mine, really played up the distinction between our natural races. And as these men from church said goodbye and left and returned to their car, they commented to each other (I learned later) how surprised they were—in a good way, a complimentary way—how smitten I seemed to be with this baby, a son that I obviously hadn't given birth to, but who was visibly the apple of my eye.

And that's what set the stage, several weeks afterward, for my meeting with one of those pastors, where I shared my confusion [slash] bewilderment [slash]—okay, anger maybe—at why I was getting the brush-off from other women that I was eager and hoping and desiring to know.

From him, then, I learned some of the unspoken, generational perspectives that were likely influencing this awkward dynamic—what was coming off to me as relational rejection and disapproval, but actually was nowhere near so petty or peevish or in any way personal. I won't go into all the details here—that's not what's important. But after sharing his explanations and opinions with me, which I was thankful to hear and finally able to understand, he gave me a little challenge, as well as a prediction: "The woman I saw sitting in that hospital room, loving that little baby back to health—you just keep being that person, just being yourself. And over time the bricks will start falling down. You'll see. Our ladies are going to want to know about you and your family, why you're doing what you're doing. They're going to hear about you, be intrigued by you, and want to come talk with you. I'm sure of it."

And you know what? They have. It's taken time, like he said. It's been a bit of a slow dance. But along the way, I've gained a valuable new love and appreciation for the beauty and complexity of black culture, of black women. And I think I've helped them learn a little more about me and where I'm coming from as well. It's been . . . not what I expected. Yet in other ways, it's been a lot better and more meaningful than I could've imagined.

And through it all, I've learned an ABC-style lesson in handling impossible situations.

Just be yourself.

You and God

(Us) Through our lives, our families, our ministry, and everything else, God keeps bringing us back to this freeing revelation: Be yourself. Let 'em see you for who you really are. Don't try to fake it. And don't think God can't use you, just because you're a long way from perfect.

I mean, sure, fight back against your flesh. Don't make excuses for being sloppy and all. But if you're not somebody who regularly rotates the canned goods in your pantry . . .

If you could only take a wild guess right now at where the new roll of masking tape you bought last weekend is currently located . . .

If a quick inventory from the back floorboard of your car might easily turn up a few old French fries, sixty cents in loose change, a box of melted crayons, and three weeks' worth of church bulletins—and if you'd be embarrassed for certain people to know some of this—

Why *is* that? Too much pressure from the world? Trying to keep up with the Joneses? Seriously, where is that coming from? Our best, most learned, most often experienced advice to give you is this: *Free up!*

Because even with all your flaws and weaknesses and quirky preferences, you are the person God designed you to be. And therefore, that's the person He's always intended to work with—the "you" through which He wants to do impossible things, spangling His glory and power all around you where everyone can see it.

So if you buck at being real, authentic, transparent, and genuine, you'll constantly be working against His best purposes for your life. You'll be more likely to push back against the inevitable sacrifices and flexibility that come along with doing the will of God, just because they might make you late to choir practice tonight or put a kink in your tennis schedule. You'll panic when Susie Q drops by, certain that she's sizing you up on the cleanliness of your countertops and whether or not everyone's bed is made, rather than you being able to stay content with who you are and how you're living your Love One priorities.

Let's get this straight: Keep the main thing the main thing. More than all the other jazz you try to keep balanced and juggled and spinning above your head, the most important by far is that you stay locked in to what Jesus is telling you to do. On a lot of days, yeah, it often means just doing a good job at the jobs that were already on your calendar. Doing your best and trying to do it with a smile. But maybe—just maybe—when the next *One* shows itself, you'll need to make some choices that other people wouldn't necessarily recommend or approve of, to do things they might think they could've handled better if they'd been doing it themselves.

But guess what? This was *your* time to respond to God's leading. And this was *your* way of being obedient. And that's exactly what He was asking you to do, whatever it ended up looking like.

Don't be embarrassed by that.

Because even though we're geared to being hypersensitive about ourselves, seeing as how we're always sharing the same body with our own heart and head space, *God* is the only one whose testimony should really concern us. If we're not everything we want to be, if we're not half as sharp as our exterior image seems to indicate, that's okay. God's not limited by our pendulum swings or the pushbacks of our body chemistry. And if we're not everything that *other* people want us to be, if we can hear their low-opinion voice in our head at multiple points throughout most days, remember: their assessment doesn't factor into God's plans for His kingdom or His plans for us.

He's the reason we're here and what we're living for. He's everything. He's all of it. And since it's not nearly so much about "me"—neither how *great* we are or how *pathetic* we are—don't let "me" get in the way of a good story. God's story. Those impossible-sounding stories.

Chapter Break

(*Suzanne*) Speaking of impossible stories—and speaking of being ourselves—we'll let you in on a little secret concerning our mind-set when we travel to set up shop at some of the various conference events we're invited to attend.

We love the opportunity to visit with people, to talk about 147, and to encourage people in their journeys toward adoption or in living out the various issues that arise. We really do love it, don't we?

(*Gwen*) Yes, we love it.

(*Suzanne*) Yes, we love it. But, um—well, we love, *too*, whenever we can break away from our ministry booth, sneak up to our hotel room, and settle in for a rare, indulgent treat in the life of a busy, bone-tired mother of many: a single night of uninterrupted sleep.

Peace and quiet.

And that's just what we were doing one night. Gwen and I had already washed our faces, changed into our PJs, and downed our sleep-inducing doses of Benadryl (a must), when I made one final trip to the bathroom to brush my teeth. But to my stunned surprise—and, I feared, to the sad delay of my full night's sleep—the commode was absolutely bubbling from the bowl like a fountain, pouring water onto the floor.

I screamed for Gwen, scrambled to the phone, and dialed the front desk for help. Ten minutes later—*ten minutes later*— no one had shown up yet to fix it. And by then, water was now seeping under the bathroom door, soaking the carpet . . . and still gushing.

Finally the guy arrived, took a panicked look at our toilet, and dove into action, while his walkie-talkie crackled with the news that guests were now reporting water dripping from the ceiling on floors five, four, three, two . . .

Oh, for goodness sake. Our blessed routine. Our long-desired date with the bed sheets. Our sweet stretch of eight full hours, two fluffy pillows, and one drowsy chapter of an unread book—all shot, all over.

Long after the Benadryl had kicked in, long after midnight, we finally fell into a new bed on another floor, having been forced to pack up all our stuff and drag it to new quarters. The people who'd seen us in action that day—with our smiles, our shirts, and our stage presence—might not have recognized the women we'd become by 1:00 a.m. Because anyone can look extraordinary in public, no matter what a sloppy mess they may be under pressure in private.

And don't act like you don't know what we're talking about.

Chapter 4

Why Not?

BRUCE WILKINSON'S *THE DREAM GIVER* is an allegorical tale about a guy named Ordinary—a Nobody who lives in the land of Familiar. He works his usual job; he goes through all the expected, accepted routines; he blends into the fabric of his surroundings; and he caps off each day by watching whatever shows up on the "box" in his den at night, for hours at a time—sometimes at his friend's house, sometimes at his parents' house—same as most every other Nobody in Familiar.

But one night, deep in sleep, he is visited by the Dream Giver, who announces that he's placed a Big Dream in Ordinary's heart—a dream that's been stirring inside him for much longer than he realizes, but is now ready to be pursued—a dream filled with excitement as well as challenge, yet sure to result in helping him discover and experience the purpose he was created for.

It's up to him, however, what he decides to do with it.

Chase it or choose to ignore it?

Go or stay? Go or stay?

What'll it be?

Eventually, over time, after cycling through a whole tangle of emotions—everything from fresh confidence to waves of raw doubt, from an awakening of hope to an unshakable sense of dissatisfaction—he decides to pack his bags and make his break from his longtime home in Familiar, leaving behind a safe, secure, settled life in order to follow the Big Dream that's waiting out there in the Unknown, in the land of promise. Despite the many risks, despite many of his own misgivings, he finally concludes that he doesn't see how he can be happy anymore, even in the snug and cozy Familiar . . . not if he can't follow his dream.

But standing between him and the next phases of his journey are a number of people known as Border Bullies—a name that sounds all sinister and gang-like, but in actuality is composed primarily of family members and friends. The people he loves the most. The ones who feel as if they can give him honest advice on what's in store for him if he keeps heading in this direction.

Now as far as *they're* concerned (most of them anyway), they're not meaning to be a voice of personal discouragement. Certainly not ridicule. Theirs is more an appeal from love, care, and protection. They've seen other Nobodies run after these headstrong delusions and ideas before. They've got the stories and memories to prove it, to tell of what happened. And from their viewpoint, it's usually not very pretty. They hate to see Ordinary getting all worked up for nothing when he could so easily and comfortably avoid putting himself in harm's way.

The Dream Giver.[1] Good book.

And for the two of us and our families, as we pursued the impossible in our own lives, few things other than Scripture—except maybe for our well-worn copies of David Platt's *Radical* and Sarah Young's *Jesus Calling*—spoke quite as clearly to us as this simple yet profound little story.

Because the Border Bullies will always oppose the impossible.

Always.

(Gwen) For us—the Oatsvalls—a lot of our experience with this kind of opposition came from people who didn't understand why we would say yes to something we couldn't afford. And when I say "we couldn't afford it," you can take that to mean . . . we COULD NOT AFFORD it. Can anybody relate to that?

So in this way, at least, everybody was dead right.

My husband is a teacher and coach at a Christian school, and he is so awesome at what he does. I don't see how I could possibly be any more proud of him or happier to see the kind of difference he makes in so many kids' lives. And I watched him, as we were following through on our "yes," do all kinds of things, and make all kinds of hardworking sacrifices and extra efforts to help raise money for our adoptions and to keep our family well provided for. He still does it faithfully today. And in my humble, biased opinion, nobody does it better.

And yet we're hardly the kind of people who get the bank manager all excited when we walk across the lobby on our way to make a deposit at the teller window. We may possess a lot of Fred Sanford in us—especially now, what with all the cast-off furniture and kids' clothes in multiple sizes that routinely show up in 30-gallon bags on our back doorstep. But we've never just walked around with wads of cash to spend any old way we want.

So when we launched out to follow God's lead toward adoption—and especially, it seemed, when God pressed us to go back to China and do it again, wanting to give Emily someone in our home who shared her own background—several of the people whose opinions rang in our ears the loudest were not too supportive in their reactions.

Unlike Suzanne, whose extended family is very close-knit, with most all of them richly involved in each other's lives, I only have a few close family members. The rest of them, for the most part, I see only on major holidays. But the ones I wanted to tell and wanted to know about what we were doing . . . most of them were just really confused. "Why, Gwen? How can you manage more than you're doing now?"

All they could seem to see, from where they were sitting, was the hardship of it, the burden of it. They saw us only adding and acquiring unnecessary stress and strain for ourselves. What they *didn't* see, though—or *wouldn't* see—was the privilege and opportunity of it, the spiritual calling of it, the grand endeavor of it.

The Big Dream.

(Suzanne) For us, however, the naysayers weren't quite as focused on the financial aspect of what we were doing or on the type of questions that start with, "Dear, are you really sure about this?" Because due to the nature of the *One* challenge that God had specifically given to us, our "yes" wasn't merely subject to being interpreted as unwise. We were really being questioned if we had heard God correctly.

So here's where, I guess, we can easily veer this discussion to talk about all kinds of things that require surrendered obedience to God—all kinds of impossible undertakings He might be leading you toward. Maybe it's the very one that's knocking on your door right now. And maybe it's been causing you to wince at whether or not your trust in God can withstand the conflict you're beginning to invite from people you care about. What do you do next when you're not only raising eyebrows and eliciting their grandmotherly concerns, but you're following God into something that they actually think is sort of . . . wrong? What do you do when you entertain an idea that is so far outside the typical box, one that's such a departure from what most people might consider to be a good choice, you find yourself rubbing folks the wrong way, even those whose faith and wisdom you truly admire and respect.

I'm thinking of things like—women who minister to prostitutes, offering them life essentials, hope-based companionship, and new employment opportunities, seeking to provide them some real alternatives to the degrading, dehumanizing work options they've chosen for themselves, kind of as the only way they can figure out how to keep their kids fed, clothed, and sheltered.

I'm thinking of teenagers or college kids whose passion for serving Christ may ruffle the feathers of some of the older set at church, who see in their gutsy, radical, spiritual energy a threat to what a lot of people classify as proper, acceptable ministry.

I'm thinking of couples with young kids who sell the house, the cars, and most of their belongings to go serve the poor and downtrodden in a disadvantaged area of the world. But they're apparently (to hear the naysayers say it) not taking into account what this total abandonment of lifestyle will mean for the safety and future of their children. Didn't they ever stop to think about that? Because in their book, this level of risk comes close to being a form of child abuse or parental neglect . . . no matter *how* the mom and dad may try to spin it as obedience to a divine tug from God.

So when you begin feeling a strong sense of conviction from Scripture or from a persistent, long-term thought that seems personally earmarked by the Holy Spirit, what do you do when it nearly scares the daylights out of you . . . and when the pushback from others is not only in the form of a question, but is practically a lecture?

Do you still go through with it?

Why?

Or why not?

In one way, I don't want to make too much of this, because I'm very aware—and Gwen is, too—how sensitive

these types of subjects can often be, especially the one that
I'm about to touch on. I hope, even in sharing very briefly
from our own experience, that I don't do anything to offend
or stir up bad feelings, because that is not my heart at all.
But based on what I hear so often in talking with people and
listening to their stories, I know for a fact how deeply this
concern—and others like it—can rest on their hearts. And
I know how often people back away from the dreams and
desires God has given them, simply because they don't want
to deal with the potential headaches of tense family discussions and disapproval.

In our case, Mike's and my confidence that God was
personally directing us to pursue the domestic adoption of
a black child—not Ethiopian, not Kenyan, not Nigerian, but
African-American . . .

Well, let's just say it didn't set too nicely with everybody.
Not that we fully expected it to. We grew up in the Deep
South, so the polarizing nature of this issue, even among certain family members, wasn't entirely lost on us. Yet this previous knowledge and awareness didn't make the discomfort of
some of those heart-to-heart conversations any easier to take,
knowing we were responsible for causing at least a baseline
level of unpleasantness and tension to creep into some of our
most special relationships.

Again, as with the tale of Ordinary, a lot of what you hear
being said in these situations is couched in legitimate concern
for your welfare. I truly believe that's what the people in
our own lives were feeling and attempting to express. Even
the ones who had the most difficulty with it, the ones who
had the hardest time seeing it and getting on board with it,
were trying (I think) to be supportive. That doesn't mean,
of course, that their objections—at least the bulk of them—
weren't laced with racial bias or that some of their responses
weren't grounded in misconception. Hard to really deny that.
Nor does it mean that we didn't need to deeply consider some

of the questions they asked and to honestly think through our answers to them as we kept moving forward through the process.

But I can tell you this. And I hope you'll find it encouraging. Because after continuing ahead with our "yes"—watching God turn the general idea of adopting black children into two little boys who are now my family's grandkids, nephews, cousins, and friends—even the people who balked and cautioned us the hardest at first would tell you their lives and perspectives have been forever changed by getting to know and love our little Joshua and Caleb. Not that it happens this way every time. We've heard of horrible family divisions that sometimes occur in the fallout. But it happens more often than you'd probably expect. And I believe, if you'll keep on following God instead of being scared off by public opinion, you'll eventually find a similar outcome taking shape for you as well. Wait and see.

One brave choice can change a lot of lives.

(Us) And that's important to remember when *you're* the one who's put yourself in the hot seat, feeling perhaps a little squeamish and unsure about everything yourself, and trying to process what you're hearing from other people without taking it all too personally. Even when others are speaking to you from compassionate-sounding voices of reason, this person on the other end of the line or on the other side of the living room *could* be coming close to thwarting your willingness to obey Jesus in that moment. And while there's obviously a lot of nuance and moving parts involved in some of these big decisions of surrender—and while the value of others' counsel is not something to toss out, as if it doesn't have any merit—let's not lose sight of the fact that doing what Jesus tells us to do is the trump card in every tug-of-war or battle of wills in life. And just because not everyone is jumping up and down with excitement and telling you they're behind you all the way—it doesn't mean the sure calling of God isn't just

as valid and in force, just the same. "A man's steps are determined by the LORD," the Bible says (Prov. 20:24), not merely by whichever side wins out in our pro-and-con listings.

So—

Just as the root motive behind all forms of prejudice and overprotective concern is generally *fear*, it's also true that the chill behind most forms of cold feet in obeying Christ is *also* fear. And when this fear is allowed to overflow the banks of our decision-making, getting worked up into a froth, interfering with the steady, encouraging stream of God's Word and His promises, we often end up either swimming for the nearest exit or just deciding not ever to step out into the Big Dream river of His purposes at all.

Instead of leading us to say yes, fear usually only leads us to say no.

Just Sayin'

A lot of times, we're not looking to obey; we're looking for an excuse. We want to be able to go home from conversations and encounters like these and say, "Well, I can't do *that*, because—like they said, I haven't thought of *this*, and *this*, and *this*, and the *other* thing . . ."

Again, maybe the points these other people make are valid issues to consider and contemplate. Maybe some of the background thoughts in your *own mind*, even—the ones that constantly keep up their loud protest against the impossible—are not totally, a hundred percent bogus. So don't run away from them. Listen to them. Be able to answer them.

But the *final* answer, even if you're seeking some healthy discernment, even if you're open to looking at things a little differently, even if the unfolding of God's will might change some of the details of what obedience and surrender may look like exactly—your final answer to Him must still be yes. Yes to God. Whatever that means. Yes to the next thing that will then lead you to the next thing.

Yes to God.

No to fear.

Remember these verses? "God has not given us a spirit of fearfulness, but one of power, love, and sound judgment" (2 Tim. 1:7). "There is no fear in love; instead, perfect love drives out fear. . . . The one who fears has not reached perfection in love" (1 John 4:18). These words aren't written in the Bible just so they'll look nice on a poster or make good lyrics for a worship song. Fear is the sworn enemy of yes. And God is here, ready and able to lead us and give us what we need. Like our friend Katie says, "I've got to listen to Jesus, and not the world."

If you were to stand up where *we* do, on stage at a conference event with a 147 Million Orphans shirt on your back, you'd be able to see the fear in people's faces just as we can see it. And even when not seeing it from that well-placed vantage point, hardly a week goes by when it doesn't show itself in some kind of conversation somewhere.

"I've thought about adopting," someone might say to us, "but it's just more than I could ever see myself doing. I'd never be able to figure out all the details and everything that goes into it. All the unpredictables and unknowns. Sweet thought, but sounds like it would probably turn into a nightmare for me."

Or, "I've wondered before about taking a mission trip, but something always scares me off about it. Besides, I only get so much vacation, and I don't know what I'd do if I came back more exhausted than when I left. And as far as thinking about going on a mission trip with my whole family—I don't think I could get everybody in my house to go for that."

So between the two of us, our lives just seem to attract these kinds of confessions and questions: "I'm intrigued by what you're talking about, ladies, but I worry about whether

I'm ready for it. I mean, what does it do to your marriage—
how does it affect that? I don't know if we're strong enough
to add that kind of pressure to our lives. And what about
your other kids—you know, your biological kids? How do *they*
handle it when you bring other children into your family?"

Excuse us. Sorry.

Trying to stifle a quick comeback.

So many things that could be said right here.

And we've just decided, why not come on out and say it?
In the past, we tried a little harder to be diplomatic. But after
this many years into it now, we don't hang back very often
from speaking our minds. So . . . here we go: If we as God's
people are here on Earth to bring glory to Him and do whatever He as our Lord commands us to do, then the best way
for us to experience our best life is by aligning ourselves with
that one, driving principle. And don't you think, if He's called
you to say yes to something that you *know* you're disobeying
by not following through on it—don't you think He's big and
good enough to know you've got a marriage and family that
are still dependent on His provision and His blessing? And
if you walk with Him in trusting surrender, don't you think
He'll fulfill His promises to you and keep you sustained
through every leg of the journey He's led you on?

From our experience, we've seen that kids can handle
whatever their *parents* choose to handle. And when they see
you getting on your knees, saying, "We know, Lord, we can't
do everything You're asking of us, but we know *You* can do it,
and we choose to follow You anyway"—then everybody will
receive what they need from Him to keep going, learning,
growing, and succeeding. When they see you making moves
to follow God's heart for the hurting, the needy, the lost, and
the lonely, watching Him use you to put smiles of hope and
belonging on people's faces, your children will start believing
they can do it, too, in their own worlds of influence.

To think otherwise—that's the fear talking.

When you dig down to the bottom of this sentiment, down where fear is calling most of the shots, you'll almost always find it worming a spirit of "no" into your life, even if your overall desire and intention is to say "yes." And that just won't do. If we know anything about serving God and living freely for Jesus, it's that He doesn't want one single "no" in our hearts, resisting what He's planning to do through our lives.

"No" is what keeps impossible things perpetually impossible.

There just can't be any "no" mingled in with our "yes." In any form. Whether it's motivated by fear or doubt or distrust or misconception, everything that resists God's complete authority to employ us and position us and stretch us—and love us—and bless us—is a fretful waste of everyone's time. So our advice to you is the same as our advice to ourselves. And it's the same advice that the Word delivers in dozens and dozens of real-life, biblical situations, from Genesis to Revelation and all the way to this very day.

Fear not.

Have no fear.

I am your God.

And I am with you.

No Fear

We hope, as you're reading through this chapter, that God's Spirit is really, really communicating truth to your heart, leading you in His tender, tenacious way to follow Him without hesitation. We pray that He's encouraging you to trust Him with your doubts and questions. We pray that He's revealing the goodness of His desires for you. We pray that He'll provide you with X-ray vision for seeing through your own and others' misconceptions. And we pray that the next time one of your loud-mouthed fears is whining in your ears, you'll want to just turn it right over your knee and give it a good whippin'.

But when we talk about fear as being the prime source of resistance from becoming a Love One kind of person, please don't hear us saying that life on the other side of your next "yes" won't include some painful, uncomfortable, sacrificial, and downright scary stuff.

You're liable to lose some friends, for example. We've learned, thankfully, that doing the next *One* thing does become more normal and natural the longer you persist in it. And the more you see God enabling you to handle things as you follow along, the more often you hear yourself saying, "If you'd have told me five years ago I'd be (fill in the blank), I would've said you were crazy." But because of that "crazy" part, not everyone's going to want to hang around you all the time and be inconvenienced by your convictions. Some of your friends will prove by their actions that they weren't really your friends after all.

You'll also risk alienating at least a handful (or more) of your family members. Visits and conversations that once were totally lighthearted and full of easy, gossipy gabbing, may now be tinged with notes of displeasure and discomfort—maybe even some looks of condescending pity, as well as certain other, subtle, telltale signs of underlying disconnect.

You'll probably be thought of, even at church, as being just a little bit too serious about the way you live your faith and how completely sold-out you've become to doing what Jesus tells you to do. Folks who used to think you were kind of cool in a grown-up popularity sort of way, may find your new devotion to loving the outcast (or whatever) as being not as much fun to pursue with you as what y'all once did together, whether it was chatting over nice coffees in trendy hangouts or tooling around to your favorite shopping places.

Are you willing to risk all that, when necessary?

Sound too scary for you?

Then again, *some* people, unfortunately, aren't scared *enough* at the risks and dangers of what surrender can mean. They think that by going to classes and reading books and leaning on the vastness of their personal experience, they can make their own selves qualified to handle whatever could result. Doesn't sound impossible to *them*. They feel like they've got it all covered. Try to convince them otherwise, talk about some of the realities that could be coming down the pike, and you can see in their eyes that they don't really believe you.

Our goal, of course—whenever doing this—is not to discourage them from moving forward with their plans. Unlike the Border Bullies, all we're trying to do is make sure they're not thinking they're strong enough, solely within themselves, to manage every eventuality on the horizon, simply because (let's say) they went to school with a deaf child in second grade, so they basically understand how to deal with one. No, they don't. *None* of us do. Until we do it.

Listen, we're all on board for studying and researching and doing one's homework before just barging into a situation without any prior knowledge of what to expect and what's likely to be required of you. But—*nothing prepares you for the day-to-day except Jesus*, all right? And sometimes, overdoing the analysis does little more than put up a wall between you and His Spirit, causing you not to be able to see the obvious because you're either overthinking the problem or overvaluing your own smarts and competence.

Like it or not, the walk of faith implies that you don't know what's around the next bend. It may be big fun, or it may be next to impossible. Either one. Or somewhere in the middle. But just because something's scary doesn't mean you need to be afraid of it. (We think we'll say that again.) *Just because something's scary doesn't mean you need to be afraid of it*—not as long as God is traveling through it with you, one new *One* moment at a time. Obedience, as we often say, trumps worst-case scenario.

We have a sweet friend Emily whose son, under a year old, has severe cerebral palsy. When they adopted him and brought him home at five months, they had no reason to think he wasn't a completely healthy baby. Everything about him, they were told, was normal, good, right down the line. But not too long afterward, things started to show themselves. Little observations about his abilities and development began to turn into questions, until tests revealed that sixty percent of his brain was basically gone, nonfunctional.

Completely unexpected. A real sock to the gut.

You can only imagine.

And that's what she gets for saying yes? That's where fighting back against fear ultimately led her? Wouldn't she have been better off listening to those people who maybe tried to warn her that she might be biting off more than she could chew?

No.

Because being true to a Love One lifestyle means if she and her husband daily surrender to the Lord and run to Him as their shelter and refuge and source of all provision, He will continually do in them what they at one time would've considered impossible. They will grow to experience Him and know Him in more intimate ways than ever before, seeing with their own two eyes that He is truly enough, always sufficient, above and beyond what they always expected. Not just because that's what the Bible says, but because it's what He's shown them in real life. And because of their new, ever-increasing depth of trust in Him, their hearts will be readied for Him to take over and transform them, leading them to heroic levels of love and sacrifice that, in His amazing way of doing things, become remarkably routine.

Yeah, that's right. She's doing the impossible now.

And it's just all in a day's work.

Doesn't mean, of course, that it's easy, that it isn't often speed-bumped with days when the next step she's asked to take seems way beyond her ability to cope. Many times we've been on the phone together, all three of us, hearing her sounding so exhausted and exasperated, crying, coming close to cursing, saying in so many words, "I just can't do this!" But then she's also been there for *us*, when *we* were the ones crying and cursing and falling completely apart. Yet when it all shakes out, when all the fireworks have been shot, love drives her (and us) back to those places where God's love can come pouring out of us again, and He surprises us with just how much He multiplies us to help meet the needs of those He's called us to care for.

Is it frightening? Yes, sometimes.

Okay—yes, a *lot* of the time.

And yet He's continually helping us not be afraid of it quite as much . . . because of the confidence each new yes is able to grow and build upon. Confidence in *Him*, and then confidence in *us*.

Him in us.

"Therefore we will not be afraid, though the earth trembles and the mountains topple into the depths of the seas, though its waters roar and foam and the mountains quake with its turmoil" (Ps. 46:2–3). "Who can separate us from the love of Christ? Can affliction or anguish or persecution or famine or nakedness or danger or sword?" (Rom. 8:35). "Whom should I fear? The LORD is the stronghold of my life—of whom should I be afraid?" (Ps. 27:1).

There's simply no place for fear in the believer's life.

And there's simply no stopping you when you stop being afraid.

We don't know, of course, what "next thing" is in your path as you submit your heart to God and commit to following Him straight on into it. But we promise you—by listening to Him instead of listening to your fears, by going forward at

His command rather than pulling backward at others' quea-
siness and concern—you'll be stepping into a path that will
ignite your faith into something more powerful than you've
ever experienced. This is no time for basing your life on the
assumed probability of what everybody else says, letting it
scare you into a perpetual cycle of procrastination, dragging
your feet to avoid daring the impossible. The dream of real
purpose is out there in front of you, disguised as your next
opportunity to love, care, and lift someone's burden in Jesus'
name.

And the only real question that's left, no matter what the
Border Bullies keep asking, is this one:

Why not?

Chapter Break

(Suzanne) Yes, why not? Why won't you? Or—how'd you put it, Gwen? You know, when we were down in Haiti?

(Gwen) You mean with Lisa? I think I said, "What are you going to do when you get before Jesus, and He says, 'Why didn't you do that?' Are you going to tell Him you needed a wider gate?"

(Suzanne) Yeah. Yeah, that was it. The deal was, we had taken a friend of ours (author and speaker Lisa Harper) down to Haiti to meet a little girl we'd heard about. We'd been meeting with Lisa regularly for months, after the sad disappointment of watching her plans for a domestic adoption fall through. She had decided, after that experience, to opt for an international adoption. And to look at special-needs.

(Gwen) So when we got there and saw the girl (her name was Missy), Suzanne and I went immediately into full assessment mode, starting at her head. Okay, her hair was more singed than curly, indicating malnourishment. Her face was dotted with molluscum warts. Treatable. Her breathing gave off hints of TB. That can be handled with medication. And her teeth—rotten, decayed. But that's okay, too. They're just teeth. A child's teeth can still grow in, or there are always cosmetic options, so—

(Suzanne) It was about this time that I turned to look at Lisa, expecting to see our confidence rubbing off on her. *It wasn't.* Something about the teeth especially—the rotting teeth—caused her breath to slow, her head to swoon. It all might've looked manageable to *us*, but it sure didn't look manageable to her. And you could see it all over her face. "It's okay, Lisa. It's okay," I said. "We'll help you take care of *all* of this. We're not going to leave you to deal with it alone." Compassion, encouragement. That was my plan.

And then came Gwen, cutting through it.

Like a drill sergeant.

(Gwen) "Hey," I said, "are you saying this gate's not wide enough for you to walk through? Because, yeah, you can turn and go the *other* way, if you want. But the other way's not Jesus. What do you think He's going to say: 'Oh, you needed the gate bigger? You needed it wider?' Come on, the gate's wide, Lisa. You going through it or not?"

(Suzanne) Oh, man. It was classic. Lisa, of course, we've sat under her Bible teaching, and she's so incredible. But on that day, in that situation, she needed what *we* could deliver— the confidence to say to her, "Why not?"

Fast-forward two years, and Missy is now at home, her HIV undetectable, traveling the world with her mother, spreading the love of Jesus. And again we say, "Why not?"

Note

1. Bruce Wilkinson, *The Dream Giver* (Colorado Springs: Multnomah, 2003).

Chapter 5

All In

PEOPLE OFTEN ASK, "HOW do you know, when you think God may be calling you to do something—how do you know if it's really Him, if it's really His will? How do you know it's not just guilt or ambition or codependency or whatever? How do you know what to do when you just . . . when you don't know for sure *what* to do?" And that's a really good question. Without a really good answer.

Because here's the thing: you probably *won't* know.

Until you're square in the middle of it.

And then—usually only then—do those doubts disappear.

Between the two of us, we've heard each other, at a few significant moments in our lives, sobbing with such guttural heaves of emotion, we never actually knew such sounds were capable of coming from a human body. The depth of desperation, the sense of sheer inadequacy, the clawing, heartbreaking realities lunging at you from all directions, one after another, just . . . terrified, terrifying. You've stepped out in what you thought to be obedience. You've put yourself and your future on the line to try doing His will, to care for another person out of your love and gratitude for Jesus. And—

Ow! Ow!

Ow! OUCH!

You're simply not equipped to deal with this. It's impossible! You have no idea what to do, and no idea what to do next after that. And even if you did, you don't know how in the world you could possibly survive it. You just cannot go on any longer.

He's pushed you too far this time. He's asked too much. Nobody should be made to stomach this level of pain and distress. The way you're feeling right now, if you could do anything you wanted, you'd run screaming back to safety as fast as your legs would carry you, and you'd never risk encountering something this painful again, ever in your life—at least not by any choice of your own. Not if you could help it.

Because apparently, from the dire look of things, you feel as though you're drowning. Everything you're thinking and feeling is saying you bought into a real miscalculation of what your spiritual signals were sending you. And you're not about to hang around now to see how much worse it could get, all right? That's it. You're out. Pulling the plug. This is *over.*

And yet . . . that's not what you end up doing.

You *do* stay. You *do* stick it out. Because . . .

Because, okay—you know what? Here's the deal. God brought you to this place, even this lonely place, by leading you from one surrendered yes to the next. You *know* that. You're *sure* of that. And because He is God, because He is sovereign, He knew this was going to happen to you before you ever even got here. Doesn't make it any easier to deal with, no. Doesn't help you understand why this is happening. Doesn't mean you can figure it all out in your head or know how to respond to what the next twenty-four hours may demand of you.

But who are *you* to say to God that you've decided you're not going to take it anymore, that you're not going to follow Him any further into this journey He's started you out on? As

much as it hurts, as bad as it is—as *impossible* as it seems—
you're going to believe His Word and His will, no matter what
the bullhorn of fear and emotion is screeching at you, both
from inside and from outside.

You're not turning back.

You're staying all-in.

And in that moment—*you know.* You know the answer
to that unanswerable question, "How do I know if God is
calling me to do this?" Here's how: because you obeyed Him
in what you *did* know. You surrendered. You said yes. And
even though the fallout has perhaps turned sideways, upside
down, or inside out, you're committed to seeing it through.
You're pressing forward. You're staying all-in. And you're still
saying yes.

Always saying yes.

That's the kind of trembling, trusting heart that can truly
hear the voice of God's Spirit . . . and know. Up until you
reach that point, you can never affirm with absolute certainty
what your soul will be able to handle, how far you'll be willing
to go to follow God's lead. But when the time arrives, when it
all comes down to a yes or a no, and you find yourself willing
to trust Him to shepherd you on through it anyway . . .

Then you'll know. He'll give you that kind of heart. The
I'll-do-anything heart. The you-just-name-it heart. The God-
gets-all-the-glory heart.

The all-in heart.

And when that green light snaps on, the most incredible kind of joy you can imagine begins pulsing through
every artery. You can feel it. The release. The freedom. The
warmth. The want-to. Even with impossibility and impatience working double-time against you, an illogical sense of
rest and peace rushes in to shock-absorb the discomfort.

And what's so cool about it is that He gives this kind
of heart to people who show up with no built-in reason for
anticipating it or dredging it up from inside. We can hardly

think of any two women who are less qualified than ourselves—from the standpoint of courage and character and
confidence and all the other apparent prerequisites—to bring
anything of value to God that He could appropriate for any
sizable purpose. And yet through this Love One pattern
of saying yes to God, yes to God, simply and with humble
submission over time—yes to God—He develops this all-in
strength and willpower within people who would otherwise
flame out at the slightest provocation.

So in the stories you're about to read, the ones we've
lived and are recapturing for you throughout this chapter,
please don't see two women and two families who are freaks
of spiritual nature, who eat spiritual-giant fiber sprinkled
directly into our breakfast cereal every morning. Because
if any of what you hear sounds impossibly heroic, it's only
because that's what God does when His people say yes. It's
what comes along with His calling—the impossible promise
He makes to any of us, to all of us—the promise that He can
turn each of us into all-in people.

Maggie

(*Gwen*) We had it all worked out. We actually thought it
was kind of fun that God had timed it up like this, so that
Suzanne and I could go through all the run-up stuff to our
second adoptions together, same as we'd done with the first.

Once everything neared the final stages, I was scheduled
to fly out to China to retrieve our new daughter, and she was
all set to stay at home and watch my kids. Then after my
return trip, when I got back, I'd swap out the favor for her.
How convenient. Everything all nicely buttoned up.

But no sooner had I landed in China, settled into my hotel
room, and snapped on my computer, I got word from Suzanne

through e-mail: the birth mother was delivering their baby earlier than expected, two time zones away.

Change of plans.

But . . . okay. No problem, she said. Between Scott, Mike, and her own sweetly persuasive form of arm-twisting, she'd made arrangements for both of our bunches to be well taken care of. Everything was back on board to start rolling again, even if not exactly as we'd planned.

Oh, how differently it would turn out than we had planned.

God had actually been calling me—starting with my first time in China, during Emily's adoption—to prepare to go back and adopt from there again. I felt very strongly (as I've mentioned before) that she needed someone in our family who shared her same history, not only in nationality but also in circumstance. Together, I reasoned, they could help each other deal with their unusual unknowns—two girls with no clue about the identity of their biological mom or dad, nor why they were ever abandoned on the steps of a government building for just anybody to raise. I could imagine them one day learning in history class about the one-child limit in China, and how girls were often devalued as a result—and yet how God had intervened to preserve them for life in a loving, caring family. I hoped they'd never be able to say, "Nobody really understands me," because they'd each have a sister who knew exactly how the other one felt.

So *that* was the first, next "yes" we felt called upon to make.

Something else, though, came along that required another yes, and revealed to me what God was seeking to grow in our hearts through this whole new undertaking. For not only had Scott and I become as convinced as possible that God wanted us to return to China, but He was also whispering His intention to us that we adopt a special-needs child.

The way it worked in those days, you'd receive a list each month of children that were available, along with a summary of their physical or mental conditions, and you'd pick the ones that you felt like you could handle. The first few times, when we made our possible selections, we leaned hard toward girls whose special needs were the most minor. After all, we felt pretty brave for being willing to adopt a special-needs child of *any* description, even if we were still sort of hoping to work within a certain range of parameters. But after being passed over for two straight months, we started to wonder what our selections were really saying. How big was our yes? And how much of it was a no?

This proved to be a real turning point for us in our relationship with the Lord—how we'd basically been putting a scale on our obedience. We'd been defining the conditions for what we'd agree to, telling Him we'd only go so far and no further. But if we really meant what "yes" is intended to mean for a follower of Christ, maybe we needed to be ready to stand back with our arms wide open, trusting that He was in full control of it all, believing that His ability to work wonders was much more all-inclusive than we'd been giving Him credit for.

So by the third month, our check box of possibles went a lot wider and deeper than ever before. They included even a girl who had no fingers, only a single thumb attached to one hand. A doctor friend of ours—someone who specializes in this area—had told us, after we'd gone to him with our questions about what a child's life would be like with this limitation, "The truth is, guys, she'll learn how to do more with that one thumb than you can do with all ten fingers." Kids, he said, are just remarkably adaptive with what seems to others an impossible constraint, especially when it's the only thing they've ever known. So we looked at each other, held our breath, and said, "Okay, then."

We're all-in.

But that's not the girl we ended up getting. That's just what God was doing to prepare us for what was coming next.

Not until another go-round of options were we finally paired with Maggie—a two-year-old child who, according to her medical records, had been burned by an inattentive aid worker while living in foster care. She had lost some skin and hair as a result, and perhaps had suffered some additional injuries, but from the best we could tell, all had been surgically repaired and replaced. Maybe it wasn't too bad. And from the look of all the cute hats, bandanas, and kerchief-style things that Suzanne and I found while browsing around on the Internet, we knew we could give that angel some adorable headwear and make her a real fashion personality. Sounded like fun.

Let's get going.

So off I went.

But from the moment I first saw her, I immediately knew I hadn't been told the half of it.

I don't know even to this day what kind of abuse Maggie had undergone . . . and was perhaps still undergoing. Her eyes were so fearful and hollow, both of them circled underneath by crimson-black bruises and discolorations. Scrapes and scars were visible all over her little body. And worst of all, looking down on the place in her skull where parts of bone and flesh had been removed due to infections from surgery, I could actually see her brain palpitating beneath the skin.

I was broken for her, and I was scared.

And still, I hadn't seen *anything* yet.

In the couple of days and nights that followed, I sat with Maggie in my hotel room, while she hit and scratched and bit and screamed and flew into violent tantrums that no amount of coaxing or cuddling could even begin to quiet into a resting calm, much less an exhausted sleep. Her eyes would roll back in her head, she'd writhe like she was in a seizure, and just go completely out-of-body, for what seemed like hours at a time.

I phoned Scott back home, wailing, panicking. I called Suzanne, who was simultaneously going through her own issues with Caleb's adoption, out in the Western U.S.—and sobbed. I cried aloud to God, begging for help, "What am I going to do, Lord? How can I get my daughter to feel safe with me? Did I not hear You right? I must *not* have. This can't be happening. It just *can't*!"

My first experience at adoption had been almost perfect. Precious from the word *go*. Naturally, I knew better than to expect I'd be so fortunate twice in a row. But still—I could never have dreamed *this*.

I was thousands of miles from home, with a terrible-two who made terrible-twos look like kittens curled up at the fireplace. And I had never felt more woefully unprepared for anything else in my life.

I'd like to say that this scene I've barely described for you was the tough adjustment phase that would gradually ease up and end by the time I finally got her home and nested under our roof. But in fact, her trauma only intensified. She didn't speak a human word for the first six months—didn't really say *anything* except scream. And at almost any motion that anyone made in her direction, she would flash with an angry fear—almost animalistic in nature. I had to tell the kids, "Don't anybody sneak a chip from Maggie's plate. Don't do anything that might intentionally, even playfully agitate her"—because she would just attack. I couldn't take her out anywhere, except to Suzanne's house, and ever expect her to climb down off of me. At church, at the store, at basketball games, and anywhere out in public, she refused—at shrieking volume—to put her feet on the ground.

She would even do this thing in her sleep—what little sleep she got, four hours a night (or day) at the outside max— where she would try to kick herself free from the end of the bed, moaning and screaming in a frenzied attempt at escape. From the best we could tell, it was a reflex she must've learned from her experiences being bound to a hospital bed, withheld pain medicine, forced to endure in personal agony the horrors of her private, excruciating hell. It was hard for me to even think about it, because I was so broken and angry about what Maggie had endured before I became her mother.

And all this inner torture of hers now became ours.

Became mine.

It went on like this for days. And weeks. And months. And never got any better. Because not only were we dealing with this hair-trigger of frightening irritation and retaliation, but I was also driving her to the hospital twice a week for the doctors to fashion and inflate special implants in her injured head. The material they used was sort of like a balloon, designed to help stretch her good skin over the bad, so that one day when surgeons could replace the missing portion of her skull with other bone tissue from her ribs, they'd be able to cover the wound with her own healthy skin. For right now, though, these things just looked like big tumors popping out of her head.

So it was painful. And a long process. Months and months and months, mounting up to a total of eight restorative surgeries. In some ways, each procedure and recovery period helped to strengthen her trust in me and cement the bond between us, helping her grow less reactive and sensitive to the touch. I was there in the hospital every day. Never left her side. And every time she woke up to see her mother close by her bed, she seemed to shed another thin layer of fear from around her troubled heart.

And yet, we were still a long way from turning the corner. Her demeanor remained highly unstable. People just quit coming around. I'd show up practically in my pajamas at the boys' basketball games, completely distressed and over-wrought with my responsibilities, and could feel the stares and avoidance from most everybody around. Suzanne, of course, was like a rock—no matter how many times Maggie bit her little Joshua. Her friendship was sometimes my only source of relief. My active, fun-filled world that I had so enjoyed living inside had basically shrunk down to one darkened room, studded by a little girl's piercing screams, and promising nothing else but more of the same, should the night allow even a small handful of real sleeping hours.

I recall someone saying to me, at one of the most acute points in this ordeal, "Gwen, you just have to survive. Give it, oh—eighteen months, and I'm sure you'll see things take a turn for the better."

Eighteen months? Is that what she said? Eighteen months? Does she know how much time is encircled by eighteen months? Whole government administrations can be voted out and turned over in less than eighteen months. Two entire seasons of *The Biggest Loser* can wrap up, start again, linger through a long, boring winter, and then wrap a second time within eighteen months. Most women can't even hold on to a single hairstyle for eighteen months without swapping it for something that's less trouble and can shampoo out if they don't end up liking it the way they thought they would.

Eighteen months? Eighteen months?

I can't *do* this for *eighteen months!*

If while you're reading this, if you're trying to put yourself in my place and feel how it must have felt, feel the middle-of-the-night fatigue of a crypt keeper-looking woman. Feel the pounding of my daughter's tortured screams falling almost numbly on my weakened heart. And feel the Lord standing there, waiting, as the panting of my prayer and my breath slowed to a slightly more measured, less frantic, not so volatile pitch. Because that's about what it felt like when His Spirit helped me realize that Scripture never said anything about giving me "eighteen months." All He'd really said—and all I really needed to know—was that He was giving me "today." He would always be enough for me . . . today.

"But God," I sort of cried out, "I don't see any end to what's happening here. Today, tomorrow, I just really don't know. This could go on now for the rest of my life!"

And that's when—for the first and only time ever—I experienced what seemed like (and what I truly believed to be) the audible voice of God, saying these very words: *"If I need you to sit on the edge of this bed with her for the rest of your life, will you do it?"*

Whoa.

I don't know how to adequately describe the surge of raw energy I felt when God lovingly placed that thought on my heart. I was like, "Okay then. Okay. Okay then, Lord—okay. For *You*, I can do this. Yes, for *You*, Lord, I can get up again in the morning, no matter how exhausted I feel, and know for a fact that You're going to give me enough to make it through the rest of the day. I still maintain that I cannot do this—and I certainly can't do it for the rest of my life. But I will do it for You, Lord, and I will be *You* to her."

And in that moment of sheer exhilaration from the Lord, I realized that what my Maggie needed most wasn't me or Scott, wasn't her new brothers or her sister—she just needed Jesus. And by letting Him love her unconditionally through me, I could be Him to her.

And that's all I've ever wanted to do, ever since—with *any* of my children.

Because that's when I knew—I mean, *really* knew—this is God's calling for me.

If I didn't know it before, I knew it then.

And it's all I've ever needed to know.

JosieLove

(Suzanne) Don't you just love her? My friend Gwen? And don't you just love how God can meet us in our darkest

moments, and not only give us what we need in order to survive, but even give us enough so we can keep giving out to others . . . in Love One strength and mercy?

He is so precious. And so, so full of power.

In fact, if it hadn't been for these same qualities at work in Mike's and my life, we wouldn't be standing here today with our eclectic mix of seven kids. Oh, we'd probably have the first five. Maybe even the sixth. But definitely not #7, whose arrival in our lives has taught us so much about God's love, God's grace, and the all-around blessings of being all-in.

To tell you the truth, after we'd brought Caleb home from out west, which evened up our sibling genders at three apiece, just about the only thing compelling me to want to adopt again was a little girl's name that I'd always thought I wanted to give to a daughter. We already had our Grace and Annabelle and MillerAnne, sandwiched top and bottom around our oldest son, Michael. But for some reason, the name "JosieLove" had wormed its way into my consciousness, and—I don't know, have you ever just heard or thought of a person's name that somehow struck you as being so incredibly, cleverly cute and fun?

JosieLove.

I just loved it.

And so one day when Katie was over at the house, and while the flow of conversation at one point was apparently splashing around in that general stream of thought, I just happened to mention in passing that if we were ever to adopt again—and if it ended up being a girl—I would love to name her . . . you know . . .

I could tell, almost as soon as I'd said it, something sparkled from behind Katie's eyes. She gazed away for a second, then back at me, a cute little grin crinkling up on her face. Then she hopped up, scooted over to the computer, clicked a few keys, and spun it a half-turn toward where I was standing so I could see the full screen. "This is Josephine," she said. "She's in Uganda."

"Okay, hold on a sec," I said, "I didn't really mean . . ."

"I know, I know, Suzanne. But let me just tell you about her."

Katie, let's be quick to acknowledge, is a huge proponent of keeping kids in their own culture. The ministry she performs in Africa is not the work of a know-it-all American, swooping down on a needy people with her self-superior ideas, trying to rescue them from themselves. Her desire, whenever possible, is for orphaned boys and girls to be united with Ugandan families, preferably with their own aunts or uncles or grandparents or some distant relative. She believes, rightly so, in bettering the culture where she's serving, not replacing it with somebody else's.

But this little girl, Josephine, had absolutely nobody. She lived there in the children's home, just below where Katie lived. And often at nighttime, Katie would hear her crying in the darkness, and would go down to give her an aspirin, a banana, just kind of take care of her. While it's not hard for *anyone* to find a soft spot in Katie's heart, little Josephine had been able to snuggle into a very special one. And so she was just wondering, as she sat there in my kitchen, if maybe her "Josie" could find a daughter's place in mine.

What're you going to do, huh?

With friends like that.

A number of months later—surprise, surprise—we went over to get her. I admit, I wasn't quite as excited as perhaps I'd been on that first, spontaneous day when Katie had first showed her to me online, introducing her as the ideal answer to my JosieLove dilemma. Because in the meantime, we had actually been over there once already to meet her, taking along our oldest daughter, Grace, to be part of the experience. Josephine, when we first laid eyes on her, was three and a half years old . . . and all of fifteen pounds. She couldn't walk.

She just sat or crawled around a little bit. Her drooping eyes were usually closed, and she couldn't really talk, could only squeeze out a few, sad, little moaning noises.

"But she's *in* there," Katie whispered to me. "I know it. I've seen it. I can tell." And when we got back home, Grace picked up the same refrain, telling me we *had* to do this, that we *had* to go get Josie. She even changed the backgrounds on all our computers, replacing them with Josephine's picture. She brought up the subject with irritating regularity, barely giving it a rest for breakfast, telling us she was praying every day that God would open our hearts to bring another Mayernick into the family. One time I remember her saying to me, "Mom, if she was perfect, would you go get her?" And I said, "Yes, probably—because you're driving me crazy!"

But all my reasons for saying no, when I pulled them out of the wrapping, were only concerns for how Josie would eat into my time with Mike and the other kids, how another child in the house, especially one with such limiting physical needs, would keep us from being able to do what we wanted to do. None of them could really stand up to close spiritual scrutiny.

And so we ended up going to get her.

Just like Grace and Katie said we should.

But like with Gwen and Maggie, the story was about to take a really dark turn.

It was supposedly just a routine medical exam. No biggie. We knew Josie had some challenges, obviously. She had a constant fever. Was shockingly tiny. Her little belly, such as it was, protruded from her body in a bloated kind of way. And we couldn't deny, she just smelled of infection. We'd been giving her ibuprofen and trying to help her as best we could, thinking a steady regimen of medicine and watchful care would probably be enough to get her kick-started.

But when the doctor entered from another room, and sat down with us in the gray, cinder-block office, he just came right out and said it: "Your little girl is very sick."

"Okay. What is it?"

"She's tested positive for the HIV, and for the tuberculosis."

. . . the HIV.

. . . and the tuberculosis.

Even with the odd English usage and the African accent, we had no trouble interpreting what he was saying. We only had trouble trying to process it and being willing to believe it.

AIDS? And TB?

What in the world, Mike, have we just done?

"Are you positive, doctor?" Mike asked. "Are you sure the test is conclusive?"

"There's another one we can run, yes," he said. But an hour later, it had generated the same result.

The HIV.

The tuberculosis.

Mama, meet the impossible.

Seriously, I pretty much fell all to pieces at that point. I mean, just think with me here a minute about the ramifications. Is she contagious? Is she deadly? If we take her home with us, are we subjecting all of our kids and ourselves to catching TB? Or getting AIDS? Would she ever be able to go to church? Or stay in a nursery? Or go to school? Or do anything that normal kids get to do?

But if we leave her, is she just going to die? They do well to take care of their *healthy* children around here. Does she have even a prayer of living and growing up if we don't take her home?

My Josie?

JosieLove?

Twenty-four hours later, I was *still* crying, while Mike, on the other hand—doing a much better job of holding himself together—had gotten on the computer and had been doing some research. He'd called a few friends back in the States to see if anybody knew someone we could talk to, a professional who understood what these petrifying abbreviations spelled out in real life.

We just didn't know. We'd never had a *need* to know.

But whatever we found out, did we know if we could say yes or not?

Like Gwen and I wrote earlier in the chapter, life will bring you to the point where you've got to declare: Am I telling God no? Or will I choose to tell Him yes? Up until that moment, in most cases, few of us are spiritually aware enough to be totally, one hundred percent locked down on exactly what God is instructing us to do. We think, we guess, we try our best. We pray and believe and lean on whatever kind of spiritual confirmation comes through. But when you're sitting there, like we were doing, drowning in fears and unknowns, imagining the worst—and not even sure if the *worst* is as scary as what the reality may turn out to be—that's when you typically find out for sure whether you're following God's will or just chasing your own wants and wishes.

That's when you see whether you're all-in or not.

I remember calling Gwen, of course—as natural a reaction as breathing—and telling her what we'd just found out, what we were going through. If you were to ask her today, she'd tell you she could hardly make out what I was saying, seeing as how my speech was so layered in a thick coating of grief and anguish. "Okay, God," she remembers praying, "You've got to give me a word here. My best friend's gone to pick up her daughter, and she's just found out the girl's got HIV. What do You have for me? What do I say to her? I'm completely clueless."

But as usual, God gave her more in a few words than she realized. It may not have sounded like much to her, but it sounded like tempered steel to me.

"I've got your back, Suzanne," she said.

"I've got your back."

There was a chance, of course, that we wouldn't have a choice about what to do. Josie's condition, from what I'd gathered so far, might prohibit her from even being allowed to leave the country and enter the United States. But one way or another, by the faithful love of God, I knew I had a friend who'd be waiting for me in America when I got home. And whether I showed up with Josie or showed up without her, I knew I could count on Gwen to "have my back."

And I knew, if *she* could promise, my Jesus could promise it even more.

And I knew something else, too.

Whatever it meant, I knew I was saying yes.

Static Cling

(Us) As smart and strong as any of us may think we are, we really have no idea what the future holds and how we'll react to it. *But God does.* And as you grapple and wrestle and fiddle with your life to try making it turn out better than it's been, trying to get it to line up with God's plans for you, hoping to make yourself feel more deliberate and purposeful and capable and joyful, the answer's really not as fancy as we try making it out to be.

Just go all-in.

Just cling to Him.

Sorry to spoil the twelve-week Bible study your Sunday school teacher may have been planning, but really the only secret to knowing God's will is just to say "I'm doing it, regardless."

I'm all-in.

And why not? "I will never leave you or forsake you," He's said to us (Heb. 13:5). If we truly believe Him to be true to His Word—true to *this* word—then what kind of risk are we running by going all-in?

"You are my rock and my fortress," the Bible says of Him. "You lead and guide me because of Your name" (Ps. 31:3). "I know the plans I have for you," He says, "plans for your welfare, not for disaster, to give you a future and a hope" (Jer. 29:11). "I will instruct you and teach you in the way which you should go; I will counsel you with My eye upon you" (Ps. 32:8 NASB).

Just cling to all of that.

And then you can say, as we have, with all our heart, "As for me and my house, we will serve the LORD" (Josh 24:15 NASB).

All-in, all the time.

People talk about having their "prayer time," which, of course, is an excellent thing to do. But we can't help but giggle a little bit now, whenever we hear that term, because "prayer time" for us now is just *all* the time—not because we're so super-spiritual or anything, but simply because we're trying to survive. In the carpool, in the kitchen, in the morning when our feet first hit the floor, and every single moment between then and bedtime—and beyond—we're always keeping up this running stream of prayer between ourselves and the Lord . . . because we've lost the ability to do anything *else*. If He's not there, we've got nothing. But because He *is*, we've got everything.

We can *do* this.

We can do it for You, Jesus.

And so far—as of this morning at least—neither one of us has ever collapsed and not been able to make it through the day. It's not as though we don't *feel* like fading to black sometimes, just turning away from it all and making for the beach, ducking out of this whole assignment and running for cover. But the reason we're sitting here today in a somewhat sound mind and body—the *only* reason—is because of what's happening deep inside. Underneath all the busy, bustling, getting-it-done exterior, we're just clinging to God like a beachfront homeowner in a hurricane—clinging to the only thing we know: that our God is not going *anywhere*.

So from everything we've seen and observed—from China to Uganda, north to south, east to west, and all points in between—we're convinced beyond all convincing that our God is up to every challenge He chooses to place us in. And if we'll just keep following Him there, saying yes with every little daily decision, He will build our confidence with each next step—confidence in Him, confidence in His will, and confidence that we're smack in the center of it.

That's what we've come to *know*.

It's what comes from being ALL-IN.

Chapter Break

(Gwen) The day I got Maggie was the same day Suzanne's Caleb was born. November 8. And we were both in such dire straits, in fits of desperation. Feeling it for different reasons, of course, but each of them difficult.

Separated by half a globe, but needing to talk so badly, it was the middle of the night in Suzanne's world as we were texting back and forth. She remembers Mike pulling back the bed covers from over her head, saying, "What are you doing under there?"

"I'm talking to Gwen. Leave me alone."

(Suzanne) We were both going through a lot. Trying to work it all out. Crying. Sputtering. But at one point in one of those long hours, we decided to do what we'd already been doing together for a couple of years—flip through the *Jesus Calling* app on our phones, and see what it said.

(Gwen) If you've ever read this book and used it for daily devotions, you know how dead-on appropriate the Holy Spirit seems to make it for almost every day. But the message of November 8 will always hold a special place in both of our hearts.

"Learn to appreciate difficult days," it says, written in Jesus' voice, transforming the Scripture so it sounds as if He's talking directly to you. "As you journey through rough terrain with Me, gain confidence from your knowledge that together we can handle anything."

Anything? Even *this* thing?

Oh, Lord, how I needed to hear that.

Words like these just poured over our souls that day (that night), like water splashing onto a parched desert. And in the midst of our anguish, we truly felt the hand of God holding us up.

(Suzanne) It went on: "Look back on your life and see how I've helped you through difficult days. If you're tempted

to think, 'Yes, but that was then, and this is now,' remember who I am. Although you and your circumstances may change dramatically, I remain the same throughout time and eternity. This is the basis of your confidence."[1]

(Gwen) What I'm about to say is an overstatement, I'm sure. But it's exactly the way I felt at the time. If not for those words, airmailed from heaven to us across two or three continents on November 8, I didn't know if I would live to see a November 9. And every time this date rolls around each year, we take ourselves back to that dreadful moment . . . and remember.

And worship.

Note

1. Sarah Young, *Jesus Calling* (Nashville: Thomas Nelson, 2004), November 8.

Chapter 6

Help a Sister Out

ALL RIGHT, SO JUST to sort of get back to our main point (since we've been going along now for quite a while) . . .

Our one big idea: *God is all about doing impossible things.* And not just doing them in spectacular people who look like they probably don't need His help anyway, but in down-the-middle, down-and-dirty, down-to-earth people like you, like me, like us.

Anybody.

To say it another way: God loves doing impossible things, and He doesn't need impossibly extraordinary people to do them with.

But while there's nothing at all that God *can't* do in us, as we follow along in Love One obedience, trust, faith, and surrender, there *are* some things He *won't* do—because if He did them, they'd go against His rightful interest in drawing maximum glory to Himself. Plus, He knows that even though we'd be inclined to disagree with Him up-front, they ultimately wouldn't be what was best for us either.

And leading the way, perhaps, in this overall category of what God *could* do but *won't* do—for His own wise and loving reasons—is this: He will not perform the impossible in us if we think we can *do* it all by ourselves, *keep* it all to ourselves, and *profit* from it solely ourselves. Impossible opportunities, impossible undertakings, impossible accomplishments, and impossible agendas are meant to be *shared*.

In every possible meaning of the word.

An Extra Set of Hands

Sharing the impossible. In order to get started on this subject, let's pull back for a minute and see it from wide-angle.

The big "mystery" that Paul talked about so often in the New Testament was the mystery of Christ and the gospel— that through the life, death, and resurrection of Jesus, God was bringing "everything together in the Messiah" (Eph. 1:10). No longer would Jews and Gentiles be sworn enemies of each other—the "haves" and "have-nots" of God's inherited blessing and favor—but they would be joined together as one group through the saving blood of the cross. Jesus' sacrifice for sin "tore down the dividing wall of hostility" that existed between races of men, in order to "create in Himself one new man from the two, resulting in peace" (Eph. 2:14–15).

That's a big, fat, doctrinal way of saying: *God purposely unites things.*

And therefore, one of the hallmarks of the church, from the very beginning—one of its greatest testimonies to the undeniable power of God in our midst—is the unity that's meant to exist between the many kinds of diverse people He's drawn into fellowship with Himself. "By this all people will know that you are My disciples," Jesus said, "if you have love for one another" (John 13:35).

So in thinking about why God would bother to stretch us beyond our comfortable edges, achieving things in us that overwhelm our natural capacity to produce them, one of His driving motivations is to use these impossible moments to force us to work together.

He wants us sharing the load, sharing the experience, sharing the joy.

Not doing it all alone.

Yet as most of us know—from some of our go-to catch-phrases like, "If you want something done right, you'd better do it yourself"—we don't always, very naturally, share very well . . . because we tend to think we don't need anybody. "I can do just fine by myself. Other people will only get in the middle of it and make things worse. They'll cause more problems than they fix." And so we limit what God chooses to do with us, simply because we're limiting it to what we can accomplish ourselves, with our own personal muscle and manpower, with our own two hands, our own two feet, and our own two cents' worth to try figuring it out. If it requires more than our calendar and our carload can accommodate, then we just don't see how it's ever happening.

And that's too bad—because that's where a lot of opportunities to say yes get transferred to the trash can—not because they can't be done, but because they can't be done from our available, limited allotment of resources.

Look, we understand the thinking here. And don't think we haven't thought it ourselves. But the flaws of this attitude, the weakness in this argument, come from our forgetting that God's resources are legitimately unlimited. ("The cattle on a thousand hills" and all that.) And it comes from our not grasping the value He places on every one of His people—not just us. It comes from not sharing His view for how deeply we need each other, not to mention how great He would grow in *all* our eyes once we saw Him multiply our shared efforts into something that was truly beyond us.

There were times, we'll admit, as we felt ourselves being stretched thinner than we'd ever been stretched before, when we wanted to put God on notice that we were just about at the end. Part of our mind-set up to that point had been like, "If I'm going to be the mom to all these kids, then I should be able to get everything done. And if I can't get it done, then we're just not doing it—we're pulling back, we're packing it in." But then God brought people around us that He was personally calling to assist us. And even though the do-it-all spirit inside us initially was in awe of God's provision and His calling on others' lives to serve inside our home (big shout-out here to Anna and Anna Bliss), here's just the spiritual reality of it: God *wants* us working together, intersecting our gifts and our willingness into each other's lives. It's not a failed admission of defeat or weakness on our part, but simply a celebration of unity, each of us being obedient to His prompting.

It's our *yes*.

Coming together to make an even bigger "yes."

Personally, for us, one of the sweetest examples of this principle we can imagine has been the gift of each other's friendship. We would *never* be able to live the lives we're currently living if not for the love, support, counsel, backing, time, laughter, sharing, sacrifices, phone calls, hugs, and suck-it-ups that we've given and received from each other, back and forth in both directions, all across the years. And we do mean *never*. As in, no way. God brought us together very specifically to lead each of us and our families in the direction He intended us to go. And without what the other has brought to our individual lives, we would both be far, far less than we are today.

But the math equations don't stop there. Other friends, too, have been enormously instrumental in keeping us going, multiplying our ability to say yes to God, over and over. And we know, from what they've told us in conversation and correspondence, that God has used us and our influence to do the same sort of supporting, encouraging work in their lives as well. We'd try to start listing each of these incredible people by name, but . . . you know who you are.

For while it's true—as we've mentioned—that the various implications of our choices in following the Lord have driven a number of formerly close friends and acquaintances away, the ones who've stayed, as well as the new ones God has brought around in the meantime, have become like jewels of His blessing to us. True sisters. Totally reliable, totally redemptive. Extra hands, feet, and arms. They're people we can trust with our children and know they'll be well taken care of. They're women we can be raw with, be real with, who will love us when we're not being very lovable, and who can read through our junk without judging us and making us feel like miserable failures (which can be a pretty common occurrence).

See what we mean? See why this is all part of God's plan? He never expected us to be superhuman, stoic, impenetrable walls of stability on our own. With nobody's help. He never designed us to be complete in ourselves, off on our little perfect, private islands of perseverance. A big part of the reason why any of us can ever come close to achieving any level of ongoing endurance is because of the soldiering friends He brings alongside us, supporting us while we're weak, even as we support them through their weakness in return.

As partners in pursuit of God's purposes, we are called to feed and fill into each other's lives in all kinds of geometric shapes and sizes. And then, when we receive our next *One* challenge from Him—the one that seems really, really, *really* impossible this time—we can grab each other's hands instead of throwing our own hands up in outright refusal, and say . . .

Yes.

We can do it.

Together with Him, together with them, we can do it.

Home Team

But let's dig down a little more personally, even deeper than your friends and neighbors and other dear people you've been able to grow close to, and start seeing how doing the impossible becomes more doable when you share the experience within the walls of your own home.

Forgive us just a little bit for bragging on our husbands in this regard. We know we're slightly biased. But every time we stand up on stage to speak somewhere, one of the first things we do is to praise God for giving us such strong, manly, amazing guys who are back at home making sure our thirteen kids aren't missing a beat without us.

In the early days, when we first started doing some of this traveling, we weren't always so thankful. We'd get home, slap-dog tired from being on our feet for hours on end, having kept up running conversations all day, all night, all day the next day, all weekend long, only to walk through the door after dark on Saturday to a trashed house. But in good time, we came to realize that not every woman has a man at home who's willing to give up his dibs to a few days off, just so his wife can take her ministry show on the road from time to time. And even though plates full of food scraps are strewn all over the kitchen, even though nothing much has gotten done while we've been away, everyone's at least still alive. And hopefully they've all gotten a bath for church tomorrow. So we can just keep our complaints to ourselves, because we're seeing God do things a lot more valuable in our lives and in our marriages than the proper sorting of lights and darks and the pine fresh scent of perfect hygiene.

They help us do what would be impossible otherwise.

Our husbands—like us—have made so many changes and sacrifices in order for our family to run the way God has called us to do it. They've made job choices that weren't exactly in line with the trajectory they'd always seen for themselves. They've put certain dreams on the back burner— maybe forever—so they can do what their family needs and what God is showing them to give up for the present. They've lopped off or curtailed some cherished hobbies they'd always considered to be essential to their downtime so that they can perform the role God has given them to play in pursuit of even richer game. They've made Jesus bigger in their lives than their love for other things. And He's blessed them with tender, loving relationships at home, which (God knows) will prove most valuable of all to them in the end. They've won their wife's heart and made us want to be sure they hear it and know about it often—that we see how hard they're working, and we see what they're doing to help our partnership pro- duce such impossible results.

And because of this, we and our husbands have been able to grab hold and march as one into this brave new world of "yes" opportunities, watching God do what only God can do when two people in love are two people in shared commit- ment. We've realized that life can't be just us doing our own little thing over here, and them doing their own little thing over there. It's sink or swim, baby. All hands on deck. And God has truly multiplied our efforts and enriched our rela- tionship by helping us choose to swim it out together.

But as many ways as God can use your marriage to up your shared capabilities, nothing is quite so rejuvenating and rewarding as watching it spread out through your kids.

God's reason for giving you children, you know, wasn't just because that's what people your age are supposed to do. He wants to create a long-term legacy of faith in your kids that starts from the ground up. One reason you're sharing a

home with them, in other words, is because God wants them
to own a share of the impossible.

Our adoption journeys, for example—as you've seen from
our various stories and recollections so far—have taken us
way beyond the boundaries of what we once considered viable
in our lives. But among the many tactics God has employed to
make this whole process more endurable—even wildly enjoyable—has been the liberty of sharing it among the rest of our
children. It's truly become a family affair.

We've taken them all through the Scripture, reading the
verses out loud, showing them what God has said about the
importance of this responsibility, telling them, "Isn't this a
great thing He wants us to do? Isn't it cool that we're being
called to this as a family? Sure, it's going to be really hard, and
it'll take time and money away from other things we might've
wanted to do. But at the end of the day, you'll have a new
brother or sister for life. And you'll get to be a huge part of
helping them be who God made them to be. What a privilege
and honor that is, huh?"

It sure is. And seeing the excitement in their eyes has
gone a long way toward keeping the whole thing burning
brightly in ours.

But not only has this kind of sharing helped widen the
path beneath our feet as parents, it's also provided a way to
broaden our children's faith as well, teaching them how to
trust God for things that don't come easily or routinely. It's
making them bigger, bolder people.

We've worked to keep this happening in any number of
ways. As certain ones of our kids became old enough, for
example, we brought them along on our adoptions so they
could see it all firsthand, knowing that the eyewitness memories would etch deeply into their hearts and would form like
cement around their growing belief systems. We've packed
up the others for some of our international trips, eager to
expose them to heartbreaking needs and real-world situations

where God does impossibly inspiring things to touch people's lives. And when ministry duties take us away from home by ourselves, and when some of our children (the younger ones anyway) cling to our waists and don't want us to leave, we tell them, "But aren't you thankful that Mommy's going off to help some orphans be loved and cared for?" Or in the case of some of our ministry projects, like the hospital and medical center in Haiti, we tell them, "Mommy's going to help make it where another little child like you can go the doctor and not be hurt and sick anymore. Doesn't that make you happy to think about?"

Okay, they say.

They get it. Because we keep them informed.

Homes need to be places where honest conversations and discussions like these are going on all the time, and where our kids' ceiling for what seems impossible is so far off the ground, they've quit really wondering if *anything* isn't possible—because they've seen it happening in their homes . . . and increasingly, even through their own hands.

All of our kids now are really big into how they can fund stuff, how they can think up opportunities to invest in God's work and in other people. Eleven-year-old MillerAnne, for instance—during one of our recent fund-raisers—emptied out an old wipey box, duct-taped around it, decorated it with markers, then sent it home with everybody in her school class to raise money for orphan relief. When she got it back and gave it to us, it was filled with $600.

Another one—thirteen-year-old Annabelle—asked her friends who were coming over for her birthday party not to buy her any presents, but to help her raise money to go toward purchasing a bus for a children's home in Honduras. All told, their various gifts of $15 or $20—rather than being another pair of earrings, another blank journal, another top or pajama pant or anything in between—turned into more than $300 and a huge blessing for our friends in Central America.

One of our sons—twelve-year-old Elijah—through an idea we generated on our website where you can donate your birthday online, promoted it all over the place and raised more than $1,000 this last year.

Truth is, once your heart becomes attuned to giving, your kids get a taste of God's greatness at work in them. And then your compassion and creativity can start coming out all over.

We've taken our whole families to a city park on a summer Sunday afternoon, set up a little portable grill, and served hamburgers to homeless men and women who gathered around the seductive smell of charcoal burning in the sunshine. We've turned our kitchen tables into assembly lines, making sack lunches from low-cost deli meat, chips, cookies, and bottles of water, then matched it all up with a loss-leader sale on flannel blankets at a local discount store, and made I-don't-know how many people's day, handing out a small helping of food and warmth from inside our car on a downtown street corner.

It's really not that hard.

To "Love One" is just not as impossible as it seems.

A lot of people today, for instance, are going on short-term mission trips—which is awesome. They come back changed by what they've seen, itching to *do* more and *be* more, not wanting to look at life and human need through the same two disinterested eyes any longer. But why should a mom or dad be the only one to take part in these life-changing experiences, hoping their kids somehow catch the fire when they see the pictures and hear the stories? Why not take everybody? Let everybody learn from it?

There's just something so cool that happens when whole families get back from going on a mission trip together, how they all become invested in wanting to stay involved. When the lull of everyday life would ordinarily start taking the edge off their zeal for serving and giving, there's always somebody else in the house to bring up a shared memory or to stir a new conviction. "Hey, Mom," they'll say, "could we sponsor such-and-so?" Or, "Would you help me figure out how to give some of my money to buy food for people in that village?" The kids keep inspiring the grown-ups, and the grown-ups keep inspiring the kids. Things that once seemed such an effort—getting the whole family interested in living out their faith—are now just the way the whole house hums.

What's more, the web of your sharing and influence doesn't need to stop at your own kids, but can also extend to their friends, too, as you invite them into your home and involve them in your life. Nothing makes us want to high-five the heavens more excitedly than when one of our children's friends tells us, or tells their own parents, "Oh man, I am *totally* adopting when I get older. It's not even a question anymore." They've seen the life and felt the love just by hanging around and getting a taste for how it really is. And so who knows now, as the years go by, just how many other generations of unloved orphans will be welcomed into new homes and families down the line, simply because God invited us into the fray ourselves and put other young people in our wake? Everything starts to multiply, without our even saying a word.

That's just how God does it.

Far too often, one of the first roadblocks to believing God for big things is—what?—the unpredictable, detrimental effect we're afraid our "yes" will have on the children. We can't put them at risk of getting germs, can we? We can't cut into their gymnastics schedule, can we? We can't tell them no about going to Disney World this summer, can we?

But honestly, the more likely outcome of consistently placing them within God's activity is that your kids will be forever changed by it, opened to a whole new wing of His kingdom that they'd never get to see just by going to church on Sunday and saying a quick blessing at the dinner table.

Invite the impossible into your home, and expect to see the walls blow off.

Learning to Share

Review time now: Hard things get easier when you do them with friends. Stuff you'd never feel able to handle alone could look a whole lot different if you and your spouse teamed up and made it your joint mission together. Beginning to see Jesus leading your children to serve Him with a passion will likely spark something inside your own heart as well, whatever you've allowed to grow tired and distrusting down there. As a result of truly seeking God as a family, you'll want Him and His will more than you've ever wanted anything else before.

So if you've been feeling sort of like, "I don't see what somebody like me can do; I'm just a regular person, not like those other people"—well, yeah, there's some truth to that, up to a point—not just for you, but for all of us. Left to ourselves, each of us has our days when we're no real match for the proverbial wet paper bag. But God isn't the one who places limits around us—limits that start and stop at the end of our own outstretched arms, at the end of our last nerve, at the end of what's maybe just been a really, really, super bad day.

Again, this is such a symptom of the fact that we think if *we* can't do it, then it can't be done. But the will of God is not designed for showing off how great *we* are; it's for sharing His love into others' lives so that they begin to see how great *He* is.

The impossible is always for sharing, remember?

And one of the ways you know He's calling you to do something special is because He's leading you to bring good to somebody else.

(Suzanne) I wrote in the last chapter about coming face-to-face with the frightening specter of HIV in our adoption of JosieLove, who—if I left you hanging at the end of my story—we did bring her home, after nine weeks of medical treatment for her TB, and we've watched God restore her in the meantime to full, vibrant health. But so much of our journey into education and treatment of HIV has been fueled by a desire to share life and fullness with Josie, as well as to share truth and hope with other families who are suffering along in shame or silence.

HIV, you know, comes with a heavy stigma attached, fueled by an enormous amount of misinformation. When we talk about the risk of losing friends and social relationships because of our attempts at being Love One people, try bringing home a child from Africa that some of the parents of your children's friends and classmates believe to be, like, radioactive. They'll back away quicker than a hound dog from a skunk. No more play dates for *you*, I'll tell you that.

That's why many times, parents who adopt children that are HIV-positive choose not to disclose this information with others—which, because of HIPPA regulations, they're legally allowed to do. They'll tell their other kids at home, "Your new brother or sister has HIV, and we've got it under control. There's nothing wrong with it, of course, as you know. One day, they could even be completely undetectable. But people outside our family won't understand when they hear HIV, and will treat them differently for it if they knew. So out of protection to *them* (to the little boy or girl carrying the virus), we're not going to tell. We're going to keep it a secret."

Look, my Josie is a child of the King. That's what identifies her, not a disease. I don't go around just blabbing to people, of course, that my daughter is HIV-positive, any more than I'd introduce her to everybody we meet by saying she's got diabetes or food allergies. But if I ever get a chance to bring someone up to speed on the subject, and if I can do anything to burst the bubble on this ignorant and hurtful stigma, then you can bet I'll jump at that chance all day long.

A lady in a breakout session I was leading—a professor who worked with the Centers for Disease Control—argued against me one time in support of not disclosing, comparing my held views to a parent who forces a child to carry a suit-case that's too big and heavy for them. My response to her, and to the hundred or so other people in attendance, was, "Ma'am, if my child has luggage she's not able to carry, I'll come alongside and help her with it until she's old enough to pick it up and carry it by herself. But I won't try to make her and everyone else act as if the suitcase is not there." If Josie thinks our family is forced to keep her condition a secret, all I'm really doing is equating shame to it. I'm making her feel the need to hide something that she's done nothing whatso-ever to cause. Plus, I've got six other kids to think about—and no way am I making them go around living a lie all the time, letting the darkness of hushed secrecy loom in our home. This is our family's personal choice, and each family will have to make their own.

But don't think we're not haunted by the potential rami-fications of this decision. There are any number of impossible elements to it. Not only are we subject to funny looks and inquisitive phone calls from moms who think our daughter is potentially infecting their kids—responses I've hopefully learned to handle with grace and truth—but here's something else to ponder: What is *Josie* going to think about all this when she's sixteen years old? Is she going to be upset that we told? If she becomes shunned or ostracized or made to feel unwanted as the girl with HIV, will she be quite so thankful then for what we did today?

I can't know that. Time will tell. But I do know this: If that time comes, I'll be able to show her a whole booklet of e-mails and letters from families who became willing to adopt an HIV child because of the power of Josie's story—kids who most likely would've died in their home countries if not given access to adequate medical care. And if that's not enough, she'll at least have seen with her own eyes what happens when two parents step out in faith, compassion, and integrity, following God's lead, fully trusting that He will take care of the rest.

The truth is—and I'll make this quick—the viral loads of HIV can be completely reduced to nil when battled against and maintained through proper medication. In Josie's case, she started out with huge amounts of infection in her blood. Millions. But with the right assortment of meds, custom matched to her specific needs, within nine months she became completely undetectable for HIV. So she is *not* a danger today. To anyone. And wouldn't have been anyway—even beforehand—unless she was gushing blood that somehow got into an open wound or something on another person. Barring a cure, of course, she'll never be able to wean off her protocol of medicine without the virus growing back. That's true. But no credible medical opinion would tell you that she's unsafe for life on the playground, the swimming pool, or anyplace.

She's well.

She's whole.

She's a rock star in second grade.

And more than anything, of course, the Lord—through our persistent, consistent yes—has made a loving home for one Ugandan girl who now finds her significance in Him, not in something the world puts on her.

It's just another good result of sharing the impossible together, and using it to share something valuable with others.

(Us) Dynamic, incredible lives are not just the ones that other people lead. They're the ones *every* child of God can expect to experience when we stop trying to filter God's will through the tiny sippy straw of our own personal limitations. Matter of fact, He's probably put the makings of an amazing support system and provision around you right now, even if

you're not married, even if you don't have children, even if you think the whole responsibility for saying yes to everything is all up to you.

Look around. See who inspires you. See who's available to maybe join you in praying about some stuff that God has been putting on your heart. And even if the next expression of your "yes" is a simple one-on-one with someone you can love and care for in Jesus' name—hey, that's somebody right *there* who's sharing a new moment with you.

It'll always be a stretch, of course. It's supposed to be. But with others as part of the team, your reach into God's will is never as huge a leap as it feels like.

Chapter Break

(Suzanne) Actually, we've learned to depend on each other so much, it's even impossible for local law enforcement to slow us down anymore.

(Gwen) Yeah, we were in Texas one time—had been in Dallas at a smaller event, and were making the long drive down to Austin for an even bigger event. And it had been nonstop from the minute our feet had hit the ground. So our rental car spin down the freeway was our first real chance just to hang out and talk for a while. Girl time. And we were having a *big* time, cutting up and belly laughing.

All of a sudden, we hear a siren blaring behind us. Uh oh—what are we going to do? "Quick," I said (joking!), "let's hike up our skirts a little. See if we can get out of this ticket."

(Suzanne) Uh, let's not.

I'm driving, so the policeman approaches me from behind where I'm sitting, and says, "Ma'am, did you know you're in a construction zone?"

"Well, um,"—(did I?)—"uh, y-yeah, I guess so. I mean—yes. Yes, I did. I see the orange barrels there. Yes. Construction zone. Yes."

"And did you know that the speed limit is quite a bit lower in a construction zone?"

All right, so I could see where this was going, of course. I decide the best option might be to just try changing the subject.

"We're from Tennessee, officer. And we never get to see each other. We're on our way, actually, to an adoption conference. We work to raise awareness for orphans?" (Pause for effect.) "And so . . ." (I realize now, I need to resort to begging.) "I'm sorry, sir. I'm really sorry—we had just gotten to talking, and we weren't really paying attention, and . . ."

"Yeah, I figured that much—because I'd been following you with my lights on for two or three miles, and you never slowed down at all."

Okay. He had us.

But, hey, we've still got *each other*. And as long as we stick together, and maybe try to watch out for those Texas speed traps, we'll keep tearing up the road for Jesus and letting Him multiply our efforts. Because it's good having friends. Even the ones who sometimes get you into trouble.

Chapter 7

Imagine the Impossibilities

OUR JOURNEY TOWARD ARRIVING at the concept and strategy that's now become 147 Million Orphans—our nonprofit awareness and relief ministry for the abandoned, forgotten children of the world—began, really, with just a progression of one-after-another "yes" moments.

We both had gotten two adoptions under our belts—Emily and Maggie from China; Joshua and Caleb through domestic channels. And because of the experiences we'd undergone, because of the deep sense of meaning and togetherness these decisions had brought to our family, we had come out on the other side with just an unbelievable feeling of being part of God's plan. Sure, it had been tough. We'd been challenged with staring down some mighty tall obstacles along the way. But in the end, the whole thing had been a huge, life-altering plus.

Part of what we were experiencing, we guess, was a sense of surprising accomplishment. Sort of like, wow—you know?

Because like we've been telling you—since our hearts and lives and attitudes in so many ways are nothing but a big ol' mess—the fact that God would accomplish such huge undertakings with people like us who are capable of being terribly weak and unsteady . . . amazing. Just incredibly encouraging. And hopeful feeling. Like, if He could do *that* with us, then what *else* could He do?

I mean, once you've thrown yourself into something this hard, and you're sitting there rocking in the joy and exhilaration of it, you don't want to stop there. You feel closer to God and His heart than you've ever felt in your whole life, and you never want to go back. All you want to do is just keep digging into Him. He's proven Himself good—the way He always said He was. And He's shown you through real-life experience, despite what most of us tend to think, that He's not there just to keep score and take off points for bad behavior, but to genuinely invite us more fully each day into relationship with Him. He wants us close, being loved by Him. And as His love spills over us, soaking into those dry, hacking-cough places in our heart that don't feel worthy of *anyone's* love, we're increasingly able to joyfully share His love with others, in all kinds of life-to-life ways.

Cooperating with Him and His will is just such an amazing feeling.

So in the glow of what He had done with us and what we'd been learning, we started having some dialogue together—for a year or more, probably—just kind of thinking, "What's next? Where do we go with this passion for orphans that God has placed inside of us?" Because that's how we've discovered He operates in people's lives. He keeps taking us from place to place, from opportunity to opportunity, building on the last one, revealing more of Himself to us at every turn.

What we mean is, His will is not a stationary target, an X on a treasure map that we hunt for and crawl after, and then—once we finally reach it—we sit on that spot and spend the rest of our lives just camped there. Job done. Following Him is a lot less destination and a lot more journey. It's not characterized by being stuck in one place but by freely moving at His lead wherever He takes us next. Always rolling forward with Him. Staying active with Him. Listening and watching, remaining a living part of His all-wise, all-loving plans for the kingdom.

Again, to keep it in the language of this book, it's *One* yes leading to *another* yes, followed by the next yes, followed by the next yes after that. In our experience, we've never giant-stepped from A to double-Z, our lives completely reshaping overnight. It's always been A to B . . . B to C . . . C to D . . . and on ahead from there. Oh, maybe a few of our steps have been leap-frogs that spanned an extra letter or two, all in a single bound, but it's mostly just happened through steadily growing invitations from God, met with a steadily growing willingness to say yes, until—wonder of wonders—we look up and see that we've chewed through half the alphabet or more. We're way down here at Q or W, amazed that He's brought us this far. And we're sure you've found (or will find) the same thing to be true in your own life as well.

So after quite a while of thinking and praying, as we were settling into all these new, added responsibilities He had given us, we started to notice that people were saying, more and more, just in conversation, "I'd love to adopt, you know, I really would, but—we just don't have the money." We heard that . . . a lot.

Got pretty tired of hearing it, actually.

We'd do it, but we can't.

Oh really?

Because when you take this kind of response and think about it in a spiritually mindful context, does that ever sound like something we should be saying to God? *Thanks for thinking of me, Lord, but You'll need to go find somebody else? Maybe check back with me later?*

So if God was opening our ears to pick up this steady vibe from people—saying how they'd obey Him if they could, if they could see their way clear to afford it—then maybe that's where He was leading us. To help answer that sad refrain.

But how?

What would that look like?

(Gwen) Quick time-out here for a fun story. Don't worry, it all relates. Back when we were adopting Joseph—our son with the hearing loss—you may remember I told you how we intended to adopt both a boy *and* a girl at the same time from the same place. But when Joseph came available early, and we decided to take on the unexpected challenge of a child with his hearing issues, we laid the new daughter request to one side so we could focus solely on him.

During our initial flurry of fund-raising, however, before all these details had played out, back when we'd been in full-on mode trying to generate the money for two new adoptions, one of the things I'd done was to create a T-shirt to sell—a really cool design that featured a daisy on it. People loved it. Adding to that, we had brought over these incredible paper bead necklaces from Uganda, made from little rolls of recycled paper that are dipped in varnish and threaded onto a string. The African ladies there who've learned how to make these things, rather than resorting to prostitution or picking through local trash piles to care for their children, are an amazing story of redemption all in themselves. And the quality of their work, the beauty of those necklaces—almost as beautiful as *they* are.

Anyway—Scott and I had been pulling out all the stops to get people eager to help us, while offering them something worthwhile and desirable in return, beyond just the good feeling of giving. Scott, for example, being a coach, put together a sports clinic where kids could come learn some fundamentals and grow their athletic skills. I made T-shirts, like the one with the daisy print, while also taking a side job, doing computer work at home during off-hours when the kids were in school. We're all about "no excuses" around here—both *our* family and Suzanne's—and we Oatsvalls sure weren't going to come up short of our financial goals from lack of trying. I mean, the money you need for these kinds of things sort of does fall out of the sky, because God is always faithful to provide for whatever He prompts in us. But it's not going to fall out of the sky without some effort.

Somewhere through this period of time, however, is when we found out about the change in available children, about Joseph's hearing condition, and all of that. It's also when we made the decision to go get him just by himself.

But shortly before we were scheduled to leave for Africa to pick him up, we received a phone call that said a daughter was now available to us as well. "Yeah, that's great, but—you know what's happened here," we said, "with Joseph and everything. So we've decided just to . . ."

That was *our* plan. We'd come up with *our* plan.

And our plan at that moment was a *no.*

But guess what this little Ugandan girl's name was—maybe the only girl with that name in the whole country, for all we knew? Her given African name was . . .

Daisy.

Like the daisy on my T-shirt.

And like cool water running over tired hands, after you've been out working in the yard pulling weeds on a hot summer day, the rush of release we felt from God's Spirit at that moment sent this immediate flood of refreshment into our hearts. On a dime, we went from "No, I don't think so" to "Oh, I cannot wait to meet her." Because God had been designing her for us all along, and we just didn't know it.

(Us) But speaking of T-shirts, God had already been giving us these creative ideas for how to raise money for adoptions, which we had put into action while seeking help for some of our *own* adoptions. And we'd seen how these things

created a real buzz around the whole experience, how it got people talking and thinking and doing more than just giving $20 or $25 to a friend for a good cause.

And—dare we say it—we'd gotten pretty good at it. We'd learned what works and what doesn't work. We'd figured out some of the ways to get the most bang for your buck. So building on the observations we'd made from trial and error, and realizing what a huge obstacle that money often becomes in a family's decision about whether to adopt or not, we decided, "Hey, let's just create a little store, a little selection of merchandise. We'll start with shirts and necklaces, and see where it goes from there. We'll use it to make some money that can go toward feeding some kids in Uganda through Katie's ministry, and we'll help families fund-raise for their own adoptions at the same time." Love it.

And that became part of our new mission.

That's our first goal—lowering the financial hurdle.

Second, we also want our stuff to create general awareness about the enormous, global problem of unwanted children, as well as the opportunity for God's people to seize both the moment and the biblical mandate to joyfully, courageously counteract it. And boy, does the simple, haunting phrase "147 Million Orphans" ever do that. It starts conversations. It gets people thinking. Heaven only knows what God's Spirit can cause to occur when people come across someone wearing our apparel at the shopping mall or the fitness center or a Sunday night family picnic at church. We've put the prayer and the 100 percent cotton behind it. And the rest is confidently in His hands, to do with it whatever He sees fit.

(In small, medium, or large.)

For as the Scripture says: once people see, once they've been told, they can no longer say, "We didn't know about this" (Prov. 24:12). Once the heart has been opened, He expects us to act. He'll weigh us on that. So by presenting the stark reality of the problem, even through as simple a vehicle as a pullover T-shirt, our desire is to add a few decibels to the voice of conviction that says in people's ears, "You may not have known before. But you know now. What do you intend to do about it?"

And then the third goal of our organization—in addition to fund-raising and awareness—is to be a mission of mercy. At the beginning, our focus in this area was on bringing steady sources of food into some of the neediest places on the planet. But as God has continued to point us toward new platforms of service, we've also gotten involved in providing medicine, clean drinking water, and other needed resources for hurting populations, both in America and several strategic nations of the world. (We'll tell you more about some of our specific projects later in this chapter.) But like always, everything has been and continues to be a journey from yes to yes, from each Love One moment to the next.

The way it's supposed to be.

For all of us.

What, then, might be that next "yes" moment for you? The one that builds on what He's already begun in you? The one that's sparked by reading His Word and listening for His Spirit to make connections between the Father's heart, your own life, and the lives of others He could touch directly through your impact?

It may seem beyond you. It may feel like a step you don't want to attempt or don't feel qualified to capture. But you might just be amazed at where this next adventure could take you.

The Doctor Is In

Megan Boudreaux is a young woman—a *very* young woman—who felt a clear call of God to invest her life in the people of one little village, the Haitian community of

Gressier (pronounced GRACE-ee-ay). We learned of Megan after she'd reached out to us on Facebook, asking if we'd be willing to produce a T-shirt for her ministry that said "Free 1" on the back, since so many of the children in that area are what are known as *restaveks*—basically slaves for the families they've been given to or sold to.

Since we've made a commitment to be extra careful before partnering with people or entering into new projects—simply because we always want to be fully invested in everything we do—we dug around to see who Megan was. And among the things we discovered, believe it or not, were some online pictures of her—*with our kids*—at the children's home in Uganda, kids we would later adopt as little Mayernicks and Oatsvalls. She was even able to tell us some sweet stories about their earliest days, before they came to be part of our families—a heart tie that anchored our connection with Megan even deeper.

Cool, then—this must be a match.

Yes, we'll do it.

But maybe, we began to think, we could do more.

We had been in the process already of seeking out some new places to serve. And the beginning of our work with Megan had made us wonder if Haiti was the next direction God was leading. So we decided to go down there for a look—to see the secondary school she was operating, as well as an ongoing feeding program and a few other things. What we discovered, however, was that she was also working on building plans for a middle and high school, a community center, and—oh, she said, if she could somehow secure the funding—the construction of a medical facility to serve some of the 35,000 residents of Gressier. The makeshift clinic that she was running, housed on their compound, was incredibly limited in the services it could offer and was naturally unable to provide what the needs of the surrounding area demanded.

Might we be interested, she wondered, in helping to make her medical vision a reality?

Part of our process—again—after coming back home, was to run it through our grid of God's will and the wisest stewardship of our small operation. After all, we're still primarily just two wives, two moms, with a bunch of kids at home, wanting to be sure we're keeping our focus where it best belongs at all times during this season of our lives. We don't sign onto projects that we don't view as an extension of our first priorities or that we don't see as an ongoing relationship with a ministry partner, something we can keep building on, rather than always having to start up new things everywhere and thereby not be able to go as deeply into these communities as we want.

One thing was for sure after seeing the situation first-hand: the need for a medical center was definitely there. The nearest treatment center of the kind that Megan was proposing was a full hour-and-a-half drive away. And because of the *restavek* culture that is so pervasive there, most of the local children who need medical attention didn't have the slightest prayer of receiving it, because their families (check that: their *owners*) would never be willing to take them there or pay for it.

So just as we were beginning to pray and discuss what we thought we should do, Megan called one day with some sad news. One of the most promising kids she knew, a student in her school—a little soccer player that everybody loved—had developed a visible infection on a part of his body. And his mom, having no other choice, had carted him to the nearest and best doctor she could find. But something in the way the medical people treated his abscess, despite the apparently simple nature of the problem, caused his condition to spiral quickly out of control. Before the day was over, the infection had spiked, taken hold, and wouldn't let up.

The little boy was dead.

"Okay, that's it," we said to each other, after we'd hung up. "You know what? Not on our watch. God has put this opportunity on our plate; we trust Megan; we've watched what she's already done; and we know we're committed long-term to Haiti (because of some initiatives we'd already begun there, assisting with a couple of feeding programs). So—here we go—this is the next 'Love One' for us to say yes to. We're doing it."

And so we did.

But follow the bouncing ball of God's activity at work here. At the time when we said our initial yes to this project, the plans we were discussing called for a two-room build-ing, designed to provide basic care, expected to cost around $75,000 in construction and equipment costs. That was the figure we'd all anticipated when God had first opened the door and invited us in.

How funny.

Because in less than two weeks' time, the vision for this project had ballooned into a 6,500 square-foot *hospital*, offer-ing dentistry, prenatal care, an emergency clinic, a pharmacy, even a surgical wing. Big time.

With a much bigger price tag.

Try a quarter of a million dollars.

$250 grand!

But here's the even *bigger* point, which we feel sure you can translate and personalize to your own life. We'd been involved in enough stuff up until that time in our ministry's life cycle that the $75,000 range of fund-raising—while sig-nificant—didn't seem so incredibly out of reach to us. A few years before? Sure. Scary. But God had been steadily moving the posts on what we considered our outer limits, enough that a project in the ballpark of $75,000 now felt positioned within at least the realm of possibility.

Who were we to think, however, that His goal for us was just to be content there forever, once we'd reached a certain magnitude of dollar amount? Why should we think we'd graduated to a high enough level that we could now coast or float from here on in and no longer be pushed out to deeper water? Because a comfort zone is still a comfort zone, no matter where that comfort zone is located or how uncomfortable it might have seemed in days past. And God's expectation of us in that moment wasn't to give us a gold star for accomplishing the new ordinary, as impressive as it might sound to some. Like always, He wanted us to keep reaching for the impossible.

All six, whopping digits of it.

People asked us afterward how we did it, how we ever raised $250,000 in less than four months. We didn't. *Jesus* did. We just kept putting the word out there, communicating the importance of the hospital, talking about how the Maggies and Josephs and JosieLoves of the world are living down there in Haiti with nobody to clean their teeth or treat their sickness or give them medicine or stop their pain. We told them we still needed more money, we pulled out every stop in our fund-raising repertoire, and we prayed that God had already been stirring people's hearts, preparing them to give, and that He would line this whole thing up with His will in due time.

Wouldn't you know it, the money came in—every dollar of it—from generous people who care about kids and who trusted that their investments would be safe with us, people who knew we were putting our own selves and resources into it as well, and that every nickel would go directly where we said it would.

Today, thousands of children and families in Gressier are now a short drive or walking distance away from quality medical care whenever they need it. Lives are being saved and restored in a place that was far beyond our budget to build and support.

And God has shown us again what we should already know by now. He wants us all to be part of the impossible. And He wants us continually willing to be moved into whatever area of service He's drawing us toward next.

Something's Gotta Give

That's the kind of spirit we should always be wanting to cultivate and keep tender. God has created us and redeemed us to bring Him glory, which is exactly what happens as we love and serve others in response to His calling, as we freely give of ourselves in Jesus' name. That's our main objective here on Earth as believers. Magnifying His glory. And from one season and situation to the next, He will always be faithful to provide us opportunities to do so, if we'll be looking and listening.

But looking and listening means taking the initiative to think about somebody else besides ourselves for five minutes, rather than constantly moaning about the busy-ness of our schedule or obsessing over our hungry pursuit of the things we want, the things that keep us up to par with the people we most desire to be like.

And what we've seen—again and again—is that when we turn our gaze toward others, God will open our ears to hear something in their needs and stories that will drive us to want to get involved. And if we'll just start adding these small pieces of self-sacrifice together—laying down *One* more brick at a time—we'll soon be wrapped up in wanting to serve and help as a matter of personal calling. We'll want to start connecting the circuit between ourselves and whatever mission God is inspiring us to dive into.

Like this one, maybe.

One of our projects in Honduras is a transitional home where kids who choose to move out of the children's home that we support there—usually at around eighteen years of age—can continue to be housed and helped and patterned into the next phase of their lives. A lot of these older teens still lack the skills they need for making a smooth conversion into adulthood. Many kids their age, having nowhere else to go and nothing else to do, descend toward gang-related activities, prostitution, and other instinctual types of options, simply in an effort to survive. So our solution to this problem—after a lot of prayer, groundwork, and on-site discussions—has been to provide young people a home where an older mentor can live with them, show them how to cook and clean, make sure they get to school or to work, help them manage themselves physically, and be taught from Scripture how to grow and live spiritually.

But to truly make this program click, we need other people and families who can come alongside and support these kids, the way *any* child leaving home for college would want to be loved, helped, and prayed for. These are young almost-adults who want to do something special with their lives, and who just need a little help and guidance to get there.

Some folks step up to provide for their rent and utilities, others for their very affordable tuitions, others for their taxi money back and forth to school. But then others—by choosing to get a little more personal than simply stroking a check—build a true family relationship with them, getting to know them, becoming a regular, ongoing source of stability, friendship, encouragement, and counsel in their lives. What an incredible opportunity to make a huge difference in turning around someone's entire future.

So if somebody will say to us, "You know what? I'm open to that," then we can help you get connected, take you down to where these teens live, let you meet them and hear their stories, and then—bang!—once you've been exposed to it, a part of your heart says, "I want to help. I want to do this."

Because it feels right. *Is* right.

And each of us knows inside that God is calling us to more of this.

To *something*.

On some days, in some moods, when we're running around like crazy trying to get people to take the 147 Million Orphans issue seriously—no, we don't understand how anyone can just turn and walk away as if it's not their concern, given what God's Word so clearly says about what "pure and undefiled religion" involves (James 1:27), how the expectation of Christ-centered spirituality is to "share your bread with the hungry, to bring the poor and homeless into your house," so that "your light will shine in the darkness, and your night will be like noonday" (Isa. 58:7, 10).

At the same time, however, God's kingdom is vast and wide, and He's created each of us in amazingly unique fashion, equipping us and ordaining us to fulfill His individual purposes for our lives. So while some of us are meant to gravitate in one direction—using our time, our homes, and our voices to champion His heart for the orphans—others are obviously called by God into equally valuable arenas where His name is honored and where people are shown the love and mercy of Christ.

But even though our finite minds cannot wrap all the way around His will, even though we're not in a position to tell everyone what they're supposed to do, we do feel safe in being able to say this: Shouldn't we all at least be doing *something*?

(Suzanne) I've been on a couple of business trips with Mike, for example, where the spouses are invited to come along—you know, those corporate America deals. A lot of the people on these getaways are pulling down high six to seven figures in annual household income. And for many of them, the main appeal of the whole event is the chance to schmooze and network and make new connections. To enhance their business profile and their contact list.

Mine, on the other hand, is hopefully to find a spot where I can kick back, put on my sunglasses, pull out the book I brought with me—still bookmarked on page ten, after six weeks of trying—and chill. Or nod off. Alone. Relaxed.

But in spite of my thirst for quietness, there are always the sit-downs and lunches to attend. And invariably the small talk will meander around the table until my identity is revealed. They'll learn what I do as a wife and mom and the interesting makeup of our family of nine.

Gwen and I have learned over the years to let the Holy Spirit determine where we take the conversation from there. We sort of internally ask ourselves, "Is this a person to encourage? Or is it someone to educate?" By *encouraging*, we mean that some people are asking because they're genuinely interested, people who truly have an open heart—if not to adopt a child themselves, then maybe to assist a family financially or express their support in some other way. But by *educating*, we mean that some people are just confused or mesmerized why anyone would tackle such a thing, and we feel a responsibility to give a flesh-and-bone account of why this whole matter is so important to us. Maybe next time, when they encounter a mom like me, they'll be able to converse back and forth with better understanding.

Then at other times, depending on the demeanor of the person who's asking, we can feel a little bit of mama bear start to rile up inside us, especially when they ask things like, "Are all these children really yours?" or some such nonsense, as if we were put in their path today to be measured up and deemed worthy of their concept of family. Gwen and I, most often, will stop ourselves before we've said something smart-aleck (thankfully), and instead we try to say, "Here's my business card. Give me a call sometime, and I'd be happy to talk with you some more about it and what we do."

Smile. Be nice.

More than once, however, in some of those social, business settings I was speaking of—where you're seated at the dinner table together for a while and may likely see each other at poolside tomorrow—I'll decide to use it as an opportunity to educate. And more times than I expect, these women will come seek me out again before the vacation is over, wanting to talk, wanting to know more, intrigued by what makes us who we are, and—most important—inspired to be less concerned in the future with their busy activities, and more interested in seeking the Lord for how He wants to use them in loving and serving others. In whatever form or shape it might take.

Maybe not adoption, like us. But *something*.

Because the main reason our lives seem so impossible to some people is not because we're so other-worldly; it's just because we've intentionally dedicated ourselves and our twenty-four hours a day to this overriding purpose. And anybody who squares up with God and says, "Lord, show me what You truly want of me—through Your Word, by Your Spirit, in whatever way You choose to instruct me," that person—if they're willing to follow—will find themselves doing the same thing. They'll start lining up their days in God's direction, and will start seeing some changes of perspective that'll truly blow them away.

Just Do It

(Us) Yielding yourself to the ongoing unfolding of God's will is sure to come at a cost. Staying open to His voice on a constant basis could change the way you spend your money, change the way you plan your summers, change the way you listen to the headlines, change the way you think of other people.

But it will change lives, guaranteed.

And it will change *you*, from the inside out.

Because when God invites us deeper and deeper into the impossible, He's meaning to show us that everything He touches becomes transformed in some way. And by joining Him in this engaging work of giving and service, at whatever place He decides to plug you in today or tomorrow or the next day, you'll know He's going to use your obedient efforts to make a difference. Not immediately perhaps, not instantly visible, but certainly in the long run. Across generations. And into eternity.

So be willing to step out there—even if nobody else seems to be doing it, even if it causes conflict with your comforts, even if means being the first in your area to step up to the plate and invest the legwork. God can make you strong enough for every new challenge, so that not only are you experiencing a new depth of relationship with Him, not only are you touching people's hearts in helpful and hopeful ways, but you're creating a ripple effect of inspiration that will lead others to step out themselves. We've *seen* it—time and again—one person, one family, saying yes to the Lord, and watching a slow but steady trail of others form up around them and behind them as God works to stir up courage and a sense of calling.

So all we're kind of saying is, there just needs to be a better answer to the inclinations that come from the Holy Spirit than just . . .

No.

I don't have enough money.

No.

I don't have enough time.

No.

I don't have those kinds of skills.

No.

I don't really have much interest in that.

No.

This just can't be our default response for everything. *No, I don't. No, I can't.* Because—please try to hear this with the love we're trying to convey: If that's almost always our standard fallback, we will wake up one day and wonder how so many worthwhile endeavors got lost behind the routine, leaving us trying to cobble together a meaningful life out of moneymaking and manicure appointments and matinee movies.

There's not much there to work with.

But by starting with a simple change of head motions—going from an easy no to an eager yes—little by little, in one steady growth pattern of loving service, we're on our way to a life that truly satisfies.

That's really all there is to the impossible.

Chapter Break

(*Gwen*) Sometimes, however, it does seem impossible to keep from laughing. To keep from crying.

I'll never forget the time we were working our little display at a conference in Denver, when this guy approached the booth, carrying a little child in his arms. I'm sure you've seen setups like ours. We usually stand behind the table, our stuff showcased around us, while people come up and visit us from the front. But this man, obviously not picking up on the subtle "do not enter" vibe of the space behind the counter, kept working his way around and stepping over stuff, until he was standing back there where we were positioned, moving closer with each question.

Usually, whenever I can tell someone like this is going to take extra time to deal with, I do my best to pass them off to Suzanne.

(*Suzanne*) Usually? How about *always*, does she pass them off to me.

(*Gwen*) Okay, always. So naturally, I moved on to the next person, while with one ear I continued to hear Suzanne patiently trying to answer this man's questions and requests for information, being delivered, as I said, at close range.

Then, there was the scuffle.

The little girl in his arms, who'd been sitting there rather emotionless all this time, just suddenly, with absolutely no warning, reached out and grabbed a handful of Suzanne's hair, yanking down on it with one violent motion.

By the time I spun around to help, Suzanne was bent practically to the waist, her hair still clutched in the girl's balled-up fist—while the man holding her was doing next to nothing to stop it, almost as though he found the whole thing to be oddly fascinating. And I swear, at one point I thought I heard a menacing "heh, heh, heh" escape from the little girl's lips, a faint glint of Chucky in those piercing eyes.

When we finally broke Suzanne free, we both fell under the table, pretending to be looking for her dislodged barrette. But in reality, we were laughing so hard, we were unable to get up. And I made her swear, if we ever did stand back to our feet, not to dare look me in the eye, or I'd be busted up laughing and back on this floor again.

Oh, the things that can happen when you're out there trying to do the impossible. But you muscle through it. Whatever doesn't scalp you makes you stronger, I guess.

Chapter 8

Joy: The One Experience

(GWEN) I THINK WE'D all pretty much agree, the best things in life usually don't happen at Walmart. I'm thankful, of course, for the "everyday low prices" on socks and school supplies and small home appliances, as well as for the one-stop convenience of knowing I can probably find everything I'm looking for, all in one place. But still, there's always the enormous parking lot to navigate. There are the people you're sure to run into from your church or your past who politely, and yet crucially, slow down your in-and-out shopping agenda. Then invariably, there's the hundred thousand square-foot search for wherever in the world they keep the Diet Cokes or detergent or those little, sticky, picture-hanging hooks that peel off the wall without leaving a mark.

You've been there. You know what I'm talking about.

And yet when I look back on the various high spots in my life, one of my absolute most special memories occurred deep in the bowels of our local superstore. And for every word that's ever been uttered within those familiar mazes of shopping aisles and clothing racks—"Don't touch that!" "Put that back!" "No, we're not buying a video game." "Yes, we're almost done; quit asking me."—four of my all-time favorites will forever be colored in Walmart blue.

And I can remember it like it was yesterday.

Maggie was somewhere between three and four years old at the time. She'd been home with us for almost a year. So while certain things had started to improve in her overall sense of comfort and her emotional state in general, we were still at a fairly high level of tension and fatigue—safe enough to make a Walmart run by then, yet uneasy enough that anything could always happen. My nerve endings, like hers, had only slowly started to heal.

But while checking off the dozen or so items from my shopping list, pushing the buggy around with Maggie's little feet dangling through the caging, facing me as we walked, she suddenly—completely out of nowhere, totally unprompted—said sort of quietly, in her little-girl, broken English . . .

"Mommy, I luffa you."

It was the first time she'd ever spoken those words.

I'm sure, if nobody else around us felt the vaults of heaven open up at that moment, if nobody but me would swear that the big bank of skylights in the ceiling seemed to pop all at once like the strobe of a camera flash—surely somebody saw *something*. Because to me, it felt as though I'd just been struck by lightning. My eyes locked on hers like a guided laser, my jaw fell open, my face blushed and tingled. And somewhere in those surreal few seconds of unexpected ecstasy, I experienced something that no emotion could ever begin to contain or describe.

She had me at "I luffa you."

"I luffa you *too*, Maggie," I said with smiling excitement, once I'd finally reclaimed my voice, leaning in close to her face. Then I hugged her tight around the shoulders, beaming into those thin, childlike eyes that I could tell were so wanting to open up in trust. Because after those long days and nights of hearing little else besides her terrified shrieking, this sweet, simple statement of hers assured me that every moment of pacing and praying had been more than worth it. "Yes, I've done it for You, Jesus"—and Jesus indeed had been performing big miracles in her little heart in the process.

Instantly, I fished for the phone in my purse, desperate with delight, unable to keep the pleasure all to myself.

Scott. I had to call Scott—then I had to bolt for the front of the store when I couldn't get a strong enough cell signal, spinning the wheels on my shopping cart so quickly, it's a wonder I wasn't pulled over for speeding. But after establishing reception, standing there within full view of the thirty-six or so checkout lanes, drowning out the beeps and boops of all the made-in-USA merchandise being dragged across the UPC scanners, the three of us celebrated—in-person and by iPhone—one of the grandest, sweetest, most exhilarating moments our family had ever known.

Maggie luffa-ed her Mommy.

Enough till she could actually set it to language.

And with every word that gushed from my lips as I tried to express to my husband what my heart was wanting to say, only one word really captured it.

Joy.

How Great Our Joy

(Us) Joy is to happiness what Jesus is to Christmas.

Somewhere around early November, the lights come out and the music switches over to "Jingle Bells" and Bing Crosby and nothing else Top-40. Christmas arrives and lingers with its moods and its memories, with all the little traditions and decorations that come out of boxed storage to remind us of years past.

And when you're right there in the middle of it—when they're lighting the Advent candle every Sunday at church, when the movies and TV specials are airing every night on cable, when the kids are in full-blown excitement about what's coming up—Christmas can feel completely all-consuming. It's everywhere. It's everything.

And yet for all of Christmas's unique fun and wonder, why is there probably not a much more sinking feeling in the world than what happens almost immediately after it? Seeing the tree unplugged. Loosening the ornaments from their various branches. Spinning the twist-ties on bags of wreathes and greenery, then piling them all up at the base of the stairs, ready to go back up in the attic. No carols playing in the background on *that* day. And no little children eager to help out, not like six weeks before when they'd come running from all corners of the house to be part of the set-up.

Because happiness comes. And happiness goes.

It never hangs around.

But joy does. Like Jesus does. And though everybody knows this nasty little truth about happiness—about how fickle it is—and even though we realize how the thrill from even the highest, most enjoyable moment cannot last for more than a day or two at a time, this universal knowledge doesn't keep us from deciding to go after it again and again, as if those every-so-often feelings of happiness somehow possess everything that could truly matter in life, right in their slippery, snatch-and-grab fingers.

So this afternoon, we might try chasing it down in a new pair of boots.

Makes us happy.

And on Friday, we might take it out on a date night.

Happy goes to dinner.

But every day knows how to turn itself inside out, shaking off the residue of all its feel-good emotions, until the only thing we can think to do is to try filling up the next one—with build-your-own burritos, and beach novels, and trendy new light fixtures for the bathroom. All in an attempt to try staying . . .

Happy.

What hard, unsatisfying work *happiness* is.

There was a time in our lives—as women, as wives, as moms—when we weren't very happy . . . although God knows it wasn't because we weren't taking our best crack at it. We were always pursuing *something* to make us happy, trying to buy it or make payments on it, trying to dream it up or get over to wherever it seemed to be keeping itself. But not until God stepped in and showed us the power of *One*, at work in the surrendered heart of faith, did we start to truly understand a better way. We already *knew* about it, of course. We just didn't believe it. We hadn't been willing to let go and live like it.

So God introduced us to joy—which is not just a close *cousin* of happiness. It's not another coat in the same closet. Joy is a whole other species from happiness. It's eternal. Steady. Consistent. Undying. All-weather, all-temperature. Never goes out of style or season. Matches with every outfit. And ever since we've had it, we've been undone for anything else. What a relief to finally escape that happy-unhappy, happy-unhappy, happy-unhappy, erratic little whirlpool of spin-out disappointment.

Just give us joy. Any day.

And that's just what Jesus does.

Yes, hard, unhappy things will always happen. But still there's joy. Maddening, confusing stuff can happen. But still there's joy. Really boring, ordinary stretches of life come along. And yet there's still a baseline of joy. Even *happy* things

happen . . . then melt away . . . we miss them . . . we're sad
it's all over . . . yet still there's joy.

Always joy.

And it all goes back to what we've been saying this whole
time. It's so simple, really, even if it's not very easy. We find it
by stepping up to the line of the next challenge, or approach-
ing the next Love One interaction that stands before us, and
saying to ourselves, "Okay. I'm doing this for You, Jesus."
That's when the treasure comes . . . and comes to stay.

Sure, your plans at any given moment may call for something like getting the dishes done, answering some e-mails,
paying the bills, handling the urgent. Or you may just really
want to see the end of a TV show you've been watching or be
able to finish up your meal before it gets cold.

But your child has a concern. A friend's on the phone.
Your husband needs to unload for a little bit about some problems that are going on at work. And so you let go of whatever
else is pressing on you, just set it aside, so that you can "do
this for You, Jesus."

And whether or not you feel any happiness right then—
you may, in fact, feel decidedly *unhappy*, depending on the
circumstances—He is still sure to snowball the blessings of
your surrender over time and rolling forward. You'll realize it
in the richness of your relationships, the growth of your real-
life compassion for others, sometimes even the experience of
seeing a thought or Bible verse that "just came to you" earlier
in the week, now appearing to be tailor-made for this exact
situation in someone else's life.

And there it is again, bubbling through.

Joy.

That's because (we're often surprised to know) these
opportunities to love and serve others are often a disguise
God uses, designed to minister joy to our own hearts as well.
We think we're only doing something special for somebody
else; we think we're only giving out sacrificially to make sure

this person is getting what they need. *Martyr complex, here we come.* But in many ways, this is how God chooses to lovingly communicate to us that we've been getting too busy again, too distant from His voice—that *we're* the ones with the need for this Love One moment, every bit as much as our child, our spouse, our friend, or the person whose hunger or loneliness has stirred up Christ's compassion inside us.

Whichever way you look at it, God turns these moments into joy makers, all the way around.

And once you've learned to start thinking this way—once you've deliberately chosen surrender rather than entitlement, once that's become your new spiritual reflex, and once you've felt joy take over and outweigh everything else in your heart—joy is all you'll ever want anymore. A single taste is better than all the flavors of happiness in all the ice cream cartons in all the freezer cases in all the markets and dessert shops in town.

Who needs five-*hour* energy when you can have five-*second* energy?

We're not kidding.

What we've discovered, even on those days when our margins are pressed right up against the wall, yet we keep pushing forward, doing the next *One* thing with all the love we can find, God can always be counted on—always—to give us at least a five-second burst of full-strength joy. Every day. Seriously. Regardless of the impossibility.

Oh, you might catch us some nights, all emotionally dressed up, ready to drive off to our own little pity party somewhere. We're wanting just to be like somebody else for a little while, somebody who's not tasked with doing what we do, somebody who can squirrel away a few quiet moments to herself without even giving it a second thought—and then suddenly, staring right back at us in the mirror, maybe in the face of one of our kids, maybe in some instant blast of out-of-the-blue spiritual clarity, the heart of our calling will show up in plain sight. And we'll realize, "Oh, yeah. Okay. I see it. You're right. I'm here for Your glory, God, and—wow, thanks for reminding me, because You know how easily I forget— You really are way more than enough for me. I can't believe You let me live this life for You."

Pity party cancelled. Like always.

That's because this minimum five seconds of pure joy is sure to be back again before the invitations can go out tomorrow. And its automatic renewal of joy will be every bit as much or more amazing than the five seconds He gave us yesterday.

You may be saying, "Earth to the Orphan Ladies." You may think we're just spouting the kind of preachy, prissy language you expect to read in a Christian book. *Cute idea, y'all*—if people are gullible enough to go along for something so light and airy. But here's just the way we feel about it—and we've observed it from knowing a lot of people who either don't know Jesus at all or who resort to sidelining in Christian faith without letting the Word truly change them and make them distinctively surrendered to His will—

Here it is:

Some people don't get five seconds of real joy in their *whole lives*.

It escapes them. Never comes around. Sure, *happiness* pops in for short visits, circling in and out—here today, gone tomorrow. But *joy* never shows up. Because they're looking for it in all the wrong places. They think they can earn it. They think they deserve it. They think if they can ever attain a certain level of some goal or aspiration, joy will automatically be there waiting for them at the top. But joy is a gift. A naturally grown fruit of the Spirit. And the God who created it (and who wants all His children to have it) has determined how we can possess it, if we want it.

His way for us to have joy is through our willing submission to Him, through trusting in His good, purposeful plan for our lives. It's through being empowered to live the kind of sacrificial, Love One lifestyle that's been modeled for us by the Lord Jesus, who said in His Word, "I have spoken these things to you so that My joy may be in you and your joy may be complete" (John 15:11).

And even if we only get five seconds of it today, we'll take it. His joy is all we need.

Reach Out and Touch

But it doesn't just come from reacting.

Joy is also a product of proactive giving.

One sure way of experiencing joy—a way that ties completely into this overall idea of love and surrender and serving and helping—is the intentional act of *investing* in other people, in asking God to help you look for and find those that you can truly influence. If few things can steal and suppress joy more than trying to soak up all the oxygen each day for ourselves, few things can *produce* more joy than helping other people breathe easier in life because you're in it with them.

One person who's proven this truth to us is our friend John.

We mentioned in the last chapter that among the lines of merchandise we carry are some sewn items like clutches and bags and so forth, plus we do caps and other kinds of apparel that involve the sewing of patches onto the material. When we first started wanting to expand our selection to include these types of pieces, everybody advised us to seek out manufacturers in China or someplace, where cost-of-goods is so much cheaper. Seriously, *every* businessman tells us that— still today. But we want all the things we touch through our organization to be an opportunity for God to get huge glory for it and to bless people's lives in as many ways as possible. And that meant we weren't about to look at this expansion of

our 147 gear as purely a turnkey outsourcing contract, strictly
bottom-line business. If we were going to do this, it would be
ministry through and through.

So we called around and made contact with a free enter-
prise program that a local university operates in our city, and
they connected us with John, a Sudanese by birth whose skills
included the kind of tailoring work we were needing to hire.

John is actually one of the Lost Boys (you've probably heard of them), large numbers of Sudanese who were
displaced from their homeland during long periods of civil
unrest there. He was only eight or nine years old when he fled
Sudan, eventually ending up in Egypt, where he somehow
signed up to fight on behalf of the United States during the
first Gulf War. As a result of his military service, he was later
able to come live in America as a citizen, where he currently
works a day job at a uniform factory. And because of God
bringing together our need for help with John's skill for sewing, he now does all our hand-sewn textile production from
his home. We arranged for the donation of $3,000 worth of
sewing machine equipment, which he uses to make all our
bags while also teaching his craft to other area refugees at the
same time.

What a hard worker he is. And what incredible work he
does. And when we look at the opportunity God has given us
to invest in someone who needed a chance—not as a charity
case, but someone we're privileged to call an essential partner,
helping out in our Father's business—we consider the decision to work with a local tradesman to be a total home run
for Jesus.

And a source of ongoing joy for us.

Another example is Raul. He's one of the guys in
Honduras who lives in the transition home we described earlier, mentoring young kids who've left the children's home but
are now attending college to learn how to make a solid living.
He's our project operations manager there on the ground.

When we first met Raul, he was serving as an English translator during one of our trips to Honduras. But his primary emphasis and occupation was as a mixed martial arts (MMA) fighter, one of the best in Central America. And that sideline of work truly suited his upbringing and personality. He grew up in the streets—rough and tumble, an everyday dogfight for survival—and he wore that hard edge on his face, in his eyes, all over him. Tough guy. Raw.

But one of the men who'd come along from America on that particular mission trip had formerly worked in prison ministry, and—unlike most people, probably—he wasn't intimidated by Raul's leathery exterior. During the week, their easy banter turned into some frank discussions about Christian faith. Raul also watched firsthand as this gentleman, when sharing Christ with the villagers, would routinely ask if he could wash their feet as an act of Christian service to them. *Odd*, he thought. *Who does something like that?* But at the end of the day, as they were wrapping up, the man asked Raul if he'd allow a simple favor: Would he take off his shoes, sit down, and let him wash *his* feet as well?

At that, the dam broke. Tears that had never spilled before from Raul's hardened eyes—having all been burned away by years and years of anger, their ashes stored up for a lifetime in his bitter, vengeful heart—all came pouring out in a torrent of Holy Spirit-inspired release. And in a split second, this muscle-bound fighter with the heart of stone was immediately given (as Ezekiel 36:26 puts it) a "heart of flesh" instead.

Raul, like John, is another home run. A championship prize in God's trophy case. He's even opened his own gym down there in Honduras where he trains young fighters in the scrappy art of MMA . . . and teaches them a thing or two about Jesus while he's at it.

And we just sit back and go, "Okay, God, we know the score here. *We're* the ones who get the biggest blessing from all this." We see Him turn our investment in folks like Raul into a changed heart, then turn it into even more blessing to the kids and people there.

It's so unreal.

And such a joy.

The whole story, really, of how we became so deeply involved in Honduras has been just an all-around joy, from the very beginning till now—and we intend our relationships there to remain that way for many years to come. Initially, our opportunity in the area centered around Coppromé, a children's home located in the city of El Progreso. We'd helped provide them with food, education, and medical teams to serve there multiple times each year. Coppromé is led so capably by Sister Teresita, who's become such a good friend and partner in ministry.

But one day, through one conversation, the Lord took our connection with these dear people to another level, and—despite all the hard work it's involved ever since—has taken our joy level off the charts.

One of our board members, Ty Hasty, who doubles as our coordinator in Honduras, as well as running his own real estate development company here in Tennessee, was down there on one of his first serving trips with his sister Rhonda. She had gotten Sister Teresita to tell him about a group of homeless people who'd been displaced from the city by the local government. These villagers had been deemed an eyesore (which would be almost funny, if it weren't so sad, since the entire region is so woefully poverty-stricken) and had been deposited in a sugarcane field, out in the middle of nowhere . . . with *nothing*. Just themselves and their families.

The concern, honestly, from Sister Teresita's part, was that these people were just going to die. There really wasn't much other scenario to contemplate, given the situation. They were stuck out there with only the barest of shelter, forced to bathe and drink from the same river they went to the bathroom in. They had no transportation back and forth into the city, and no access to even the basics of civilization. Nothing to do but to get sick, lie down, and give up.

Hopeless.

So while this wasn't exactly an orphan situation, while the category of need wasn't exactly in our wheelhouse of ministry, the children in these families were orphans waiting to happen. And God, in making us aware of their plight, was about to take our "yes" beyond the border of what had become typical for us, urging us to follow His lead in preserving and empowering these families, putting tools in their hands to help them fight back.

In just the few years since, God has used our presence there, along with Ty's building skills, along with many hardworking groups of short-termers, along with generous giving by many helpful supporters and several other ministries—and along with the villagers themselves, whose survivalism and initiative have been sparked to new heights in the process—to accomplish one goal after another on the way to resurrecting their dashed existence.

Through our ministry and the work of several others we serve alongside, the people of Mt. Olivos now have a new well to provide them with clean water. The property in their settlement area has been secured, and they have new, solid homes for all twenty-eight of their families, replacing their makeshift lean-tos. They have a school, which the government has officially accredited, enabling them to build and expand its service for nearby communities. They're discovering sustainable job options—such as woodworking, sewing, jewelry making—energized by a new electrical generator that allows the men who labor in town through the day to come home and work into the evening. The people are making crafts. They're setting up a marketplace for the commerce of their goods. They've bought chickens and pigs and are growing their own livestock. They'll soon have a working septic system to further establish the health and longevity of their village.

They have hope.

They have a future.

They're healthy. They're busy.

They have Jesus. And want more of Him.

They are changing the shape of generations.

And like those grateful churches in the New Testament who gave to others out of their need, they even want to help us go start this same kind of program in *other* villages, because they want to be part of helping *other* people thrive—and because they want to experience some of the same joy we feel in being around and among them.

As Ty wrote to us in a recent text, "Ain't this the best thing ever?"

It sure is.

The greatest fear of any Christian, ultimately—even if it doesn't always show itself visibly—is the fear that God would stop wanting to use us, that we've closed ourselves off to His desires and designs for us. But seeing the results of serving Him come alive and take shape in other people begins building a base of joy underneath us that only keeps growing deeper and higher as we go along.

You say, "Well, shoot, what am I ever going to need with a Sudanese tailor? When am I ever going to be in Honduras looking for someone to give a job to? Who's ever going to ask if I can help build a few dozen homes for poor villagers in need of economic relief?" But, hey—those are just a couple of *our* stories. Those are some examples that have come into play as we've worked out the Love One mentality in our *own* journey.

Like we've been saying—and hopefully have communicated well enough—God has given each of us as His children a unique life to live and a unique story to tell. The plan He's created for you, just like the plan He's created for us, is chock-full of abundant blessing and purpose all on its own, without feeling the need to stand it side by side for comparison with somebody else's.

Oh, how we want you free from feeling intimidated and outclassed by others' walks with Him, or from the other extreme as well—feeling smug in your own journey, convinced you're doing more than your share and can afford to hang back when you feel like it. The Love One lifestyle is a *principle*, not a medicine dosage, not a cookbook recipe to follow, not a specific, step-by-step instruction manual. God breathes His life into *yours*, same as He breathes His life into *ours*. And together, we get to be part of something hugely bigger than any of us could ever be alone—just by doing our individual things.

So turn the fleshing-out of this pattern over to Him, simply making yourself available to His Word and His direction as you seek Him for opportunities to invest yourself into the well-being of others. Watch and pray. Look and see. And as He continually guides you from place to place, from person to person, from now until the end of your lifetime, enjoy the promise of being fully content in Christ as you pour your life into other people.

And expect nothing less from Him than joy.

Portraits of Joy

Life will always give us something to complain about, take issue with, feel overwhelmed by, and want to worry over. Life on the happiness roller coaster includes plenty of dips and plunges that, if we let them, can run us right off the rails into pity and bitterness. But joy is what enables us to get our legs back up under us, even after encountering the g-forces of unhappy discomfort and displeasure. Joy is what changes our mind after we've decided mid-run that if we ever get off this thing alive, we are never getting back on for another ride again. *Ever.*

Actually, moments like these are what joy is made for. Because while anybody can eventually work themselves up into a better mood, back where they can see things from a little brighter perspective, only those who are living the *One* big difference are in any real position to weather life's conditions without bailing out for long periods. That's because being daily serious about loving God and loving others— even with making some huge misses and mistakes along the way—keeps us full of life experiences that openly contradict our unhappy feelings. And braced with this kind of backup, the Christian skill of being thankful in all things and content in all circumstances moves into the range of . . . you know, sounding possible.

(Suzanne) Like, I'm thankful when I realize how much different our house would look if our son Michael had never gotten any brothers. It would've been all emotion and girl stuff, where now it's tumbling and basketball and camo and boy stuff. I don't know how many nights—even though our younger guys have their own room to sleep in—that I've passed by Michael's room after dark and seen Joshua and Caleb snuggled under one arm or one leg, like little puppies lying all over each other. At a time when Michael might normally be wanting his space and not wanting to be bothered— you know, about anything besides sports and girls—he *loves* those little brothers of his. And seeing them together gives me such great joy.

(Gwen) Or like our Maggie, who recently came to know the Lord—what a delight to see her captured at such a young age by how much her Father God loves her and what Jesus has done to redeem her. But one of her first responses after receiving Christ, unlike what we might've expected, was, "Well, how are we going to be able to tell Joseph about Jesus, since he can't hear?" What sweet, unforgettable concern

in her voice. I swear, that little girl, with all we've been through—lots of unhappy moments, let me tell you—has taught me more about loving people like Jesus loves than anyone else in my life. And to hear her beginning to transfer that love so freely and genuinely to others . . . I am so incredibly thankful and joyful.

(*Suzanne*) Then there's Grace, who's leaving for college soon—our first to leave the nest. People say, "Aren't you just so sad about that?" And, yeah, I'm sure going to miss seeing her at the breakfast table in the morning and knowing she's up in her room at night. And maybe I'm being a little braver in advance than I'll be when the time comes. (Check back with me later.) But I've seen death staring me in the face through the eyes of JosieLove. I've lived through many unhappy days of wondering whether Josie will *ever* be able to go off on her own and live a normal life. So knowing that Grace is healthy, intelligent, in love with Jesus, and well prepared for this next chapter—I mean, like I said, I'm sure I could pool up in tears about it right here, right now. But more than anything, I'm just really excited for her and for the plans of God that are all set to continue and grow bigger in her life going forward. She's ready for it, which is something to be thankful for. And I'd call what I'm feeling . . . joy.

(*Gwen*) I think back to a couple of years ago when my son Elijah and I were just talking at home one day, something on the subject of adoption. At one point, I mentioned his sister Emily, the first one we adopted from China. And in a dazed few seconds in his ten-year-old mind, before logic and memory had quite caught up with his mouth, he said to me, "Emily? She's adopted?" I said, "*Yes*, son. *Chi*-na. Remember?"—before we both broke up laughing. But, man, talk about a moment when you realize the Lord has really used you to do something amazing in your kid's thinking, helping the heart of God for the orphans and the united beauty of a multicultural family blend into second nature for him. Our kids are just so accustomed to it now. It's so much a part of who they are. And if that's not reason for a great big joyful shout of hallelujah, then . . .

(Suzanne) Well, I think too—just the joy of our children knowing our home is always open to them and their friends. And because of that, our houses are quite often a more diverse stew of races, ages, and cultures than even when it's only our children here by themselves. The fun of watching the younger ones feel tall and accepted around all the older ones, and the older ones showing big-sibling care and compassion for the younger ones—it's so heartening and encouraging to watch. It's a joy.

(Gwen) Right. I'll sometimes get a text from one of our older son Jeremiah's friends, saying, "My mama can't get me from school today. Can I ride home with you?" or "Can you take me to the game?"—and I'm not even going to have my *own son* with me as a passenger. Yet his friends and their parents trust that they're safe with us, that they can count on us, that we'll always be there to do whatever little extra they might need, just like they were one of ours. I get a lot of joy from that.

(Suzanne) And then when God has walked us through stages of life—like with our African-American adoptions or with Josie and her HIV—where some of our personal friendships have sort of dropped off . . . that's not easy. I'd always enjoyed having *lots* of friends, but sometimes I looked around and saw that my hard choices had caused some weeding to take place inside my little garden of relationships. Those have been some bittersweet times for me. It's hard to see people go. But then He's helped me to be thankful, as well, because maybe some of those folks hadn't really been people who were best for me. Maybe they needed to go on, and so did I.

(Gwen) Then there was last Friday, when I got a mid-morning call from school, saying they needed an emergency Dear Reader in Emily's classroom—a program where parents

and others show up unannounced, meant to add a little mystery and intrigue to story time for the kids, I guess. There'd been a last-second cancellation apparently, so . . . *Call Gwen, she'll do it.*

Honestly, I hate being the Dear Reader. I don't even like reading to my own kids. I know moms with big families are supposed to love it, but—just being honest against the stereotype here—I'm always happier to see them go read by themselves. Everybody's got those things in their life they just don't enjoy, right? Whether it makes sense or sounds good or not. Right? And, well . . . now you know one of mine. What's yours?

But what's more, I simply wanted that hour for something else. I *needed* that hour. I'd been *planning* on that hour. And this unwelcome assignment was coming really close to messing up my whole day.

But while I was standing outside in the hallway, waiting for my time to arrive, I found myself mindlessly filling the few moments by glancing at some of the hand-drawn projects displayed along the wall. As I scanned for Emily's poster, I finally located it among those of her other classmates, a picture and a little essay she had created to describe "The Most Important Day of My Life."

It was the day, she said, when her mom had come to get her in China. She told how her dad had stayed behind with the brothers. She related some of the other little moments she knew of that event. But the main gist of the whole story was this: "The most important day of my life was the day when I was adopted."

And the five seconds it took for me to read that paper were enough five seconds of joy to keep me going for a long, long time.

(Us) Like everyone, we each have our days when we're not completely happy. We have those afternoons when we say

to each other, "Today's just not a happy day." But do we have joy? Absolutely. Would we trade it for anything? No.

So it's okay not to be happy all the time. Actually, it's pretty unrealistic to think otherwise. But when you're more and more consistently living with only *One* thing on your upcoming agenda—the chance to love, serve, assist, and give your best to the next person or opportunity the Lord presents to you, He'll give you enough manna to make it all worth it.

He'll give you joy.

Chapter Break

One of our favorite forms of communication is texting. And even on the hardest days, God somehow turns it into a source of joy.

(Suzanne) "Die to self, die to self, die to self."

(Gwen) "I thought I was the only one saying that this morning."

(Suzanne) "No, you wouldn't believe."

(Gwen) "Right there with you, sister."

(Suzanne) "Started off with spilt milk, then an argument, then somebody lost their shoe . . ."

(Gwen) "I hear you. Change the names, change the details, and it's happening here, too."

(Suzanne) "And then I hear, last minute, about someplace I've got to be at 10:00."

(Gwen) [five words typed, but not fast enough to send before . . .]

(Suzanne) "And I was so wanting to go to hot yoga this morning."

(Gwen) "Need to call me? Can I help?"

(Suzanne) "No, I've got to go. I—"

[several transmissions deleted here for print purposes]

[names changed to protect future hurt feelings and lawsuits]

(Gwen) "Call me later. Just know I'm praying."

(Suzanne) "Thanks. Me, too."

And that's how it goes on a typical morning. The two of us talking, the two of us commiserating. The two of us feeling overwhelmed.

The two of us finding joy in this shared journey with Jesus.

Chapter 9

Love One

AND SUDDENLY, IT'S NOT so impossible anymore.

That's the conclusion we hope and pray is rattling around in your head after covering all this ground with us so far. We hope you're seeing—even if you've never seen it before—how much God loves you; how much He's rescued you from; how much He's invested in you in terms of gifting, opportunity, and purpose; and how much of eternal value He can accomplish in you, like, let's say by tomorrow at 2:30.

You don't need to sit around waiting on this. You just don't. It doesn't require advanced training and coursework. It's not pending a six-month process of getting your act together. It's simply about making a decision *right now*—as in, lay this book down for a second, mark your place, close your eyes, and say it out loud—

"The next *One*—whatever it is, Jesus—is all for You."

That's all we're talking about here. Not five, ten, twenty years from now. Not the whole master plan. Not worrying about whatever God's will might mean and require of you at some distant point in the future. Search the Scriptures and see for yourself: the great work of God in your life is wrapped up in the all too often overlooked possibility of *today*.

It's always been like that.

When the children of Israel were preparing to enter the Promised Land, Moses took time before his death to repeat God's Word and His promises to the people. Many years of wandering and backsliding and stumbling around in the wilderness had preceded this moment. (Tell us you don't know how that feels. *We* sure do.) Yet with a spirit of repentance at work in them—made available, the Bible says, through the "kindness" of God (Rom. 2:4)—Moses confidently declared to them, "*Today* you have affirmed that the LORD is your God and that you will walk in His ways, keep His statutes, commands, and ordinances, and obey Him. And *today* the LORD has affirmed that you are His special people as He promised you" (Deut. 26:17–18, emphasis added). His plans for their lives and His plan for the ages were intersecting again—as they always do—at the right-now experience of a single day. And from that new beginning and continuation point, God said He would elevate them "above all the nations He has made," making them a "holy people to the LORD your God as He promised" (v. 19).

It started (or restarted) *today*.

He would go ahead of them and prepare the way for them, and all that was basically required of them was that they follow Him. Follow His lead. Follow His command. Go where He said to go, and do what He said to do.

That was the plan for every day.

And it's never changed in all the years since.

As Jesus would later say, "Don't worry about tomorrow, because tomorrow will worry about itself" (Matt. 6:34). Instead, He told us to make our prayer each morning, simply, "Give us today our daily bread" (Matt. 6:11). That's how He chooses to operate with us; that's how He wants us cooperating with Him.

Today is what brings the impossible down to size.

And if you can't believe this truth by looking forward, try it by looking back.

The two of us—we love to look back. We love remembering just how quivery we felt at the sight of particular decisions or difficulties that now appear, in hindsight, almost anemic. What in the world were we so afraid of? Didn't God always provide? Didn't He cause things to come together and fall into place? Even if it felt rather lonely and unbearable through some of those deeper valleys, can't we see now—from this fresher perspective—just how present He was, just how wisely He was working, just how faithfully He was carrying us along in His arms?

From here we can see it. From here we can celebrate it. From here we can think back to missions impossible and see them as missions accomplished.

So why should we expect God, as we squint toward the horizon and the unknown path ahead, to veer from this same pattern we've seen up till now? Why should yesterday's no-ways be the only ones He was somehow able to pull off? Why should those things today that we can never see ourselves being capable of handling, or becoming, or even wanting—why should they suddenly be so far out of His (and our) league?

They're not.

And *today* is the difference.

The next *One* is how the impossible gets done.

That's what we've seen in our friend Michelle, who—first, let us go on record as introducing her to you as the "wind beneath our wings." She may not be the one who's up on stage or out front—and trust us, she doesn't *want* to be. But behind the scenes, she volunteers countless hours to make sure we're prepared for every speaking event, with all the logistics worked out, all the arrangements made. She manages our endless string of details, monitors our website, keeps up steady correspondence with our donors, and basically just does everything.

We *could not* do what we do without Michelle.

That is the understatement of the decade.

But long before this, before she was serving with us so faithfully here in the trenches, she started out where all of us do. On the sidelines. She'd begun feeling that first pull toward adoption—having come to that *today* moment in her journey—but didn't know what to do next. So she'd come to talk with us. Just as friends. She'd bought a shirt from us. Bought a necklace. She was continually inching closer, taking those one-by-one steps that align believing hearts with God's will, seeing where He might lead. Finally, she and her husband edged ever nearer, proceeding with plans to adopt from Uganda, having made themselves open to the idea of adding another child to their family of three girls. It wasn't a decision that happened all at once, but rather in day-by-day increments of ongoing obedience.

Then one day, after becoming paper-ready to follow through on their plans, Michelle got a phone call, asking if they would consider taking a child who was currently available for domestic adoption. *No*, she might've said. That's not how her tomorrow was supposed to go. They'd been gearing up in *another* direction, feeling more than adequately challenged in preparing to add just *one* new child to their home.

Yet she said yes anyway. She did what God was telling her to do on *that day*. And soon, all those daily decisions to obey and surrender became *two* new kids around their table, a double blessing of both responsibility and reward. *Impossible?* Yes. To some. But not to people who make saying yes a key part of their daily diet. Not to people who stay open every day to the kind of challenging fun that leads to the most unbelievable joy in the world.

So don't try avoiding whatever discomfort you may feel in how God seems to be leading you today. Stop resisting or explaining away certain passages of Scripture when God is speaking through them so personally to you, preaching to you, challenging you, wanting to see how much of yourself you're willing to give to obey Him. He's only wanting to take you to good places—places of accomplishment and relationship, places of abundance and opportunity. To joy.

Does forgiveness sound impossible? Not if you jump at the next chance to let God's love be *your* love for that person (see Col. 3:13).

Does owning up to your sins sound impossible? Does being spiritually accountable sound impossible? Not if you set a time to sit down with a mentor, a friend, your spouse, or a church leader and prepare for God's sweet freedom and healing to flow (see James 5:16).

Does putting a regular, sacrificial check in the offering plate sound impossible? Not if you start by doing it this week as an act of trusting obedience, discovering yourself contented in His provision (see Mal. 3:10).

Does being a blessing to the poor and needy feel like more than you can add to your schedule? Is it more than you can stomach with your high level of safety concerns? Not if you bust the bubble of impossibility by just going out there and making the compassionate effort *one time*, and seeing how doable and desirable it becomes (see Ps. 41:1).

Most things only seem intimidating because they're unknown. Or because we've heard horror stories. Or because they sound too confusing, or time-consuming, or complicated. Seen from a distance, they just look too imposing, problematic, unrealistic. But if God's Word is true—which it is—you don't need to make too many determined pokes at the impossible before you begin seeing some chinks in its armor. Try following it up with another attack tomorrow, then another next week, letting God habitually lead your timid heart ever deeper into your fears. And pretty soon, the growl that's always sent you scampering away from danger in days past will strangely not sound quite so ferocious anymore.

That's just how it is when we Love One.

Parents of young kids, for example, are often terrified when they think ahead to certain stages in their children's lives that they haven't experienced yet. What about when they reach puberty, for instance? What about when they move up into middle school? What about when they want to start dating? Things like that. What kind of world will they be inheriting by the time they leave home? How is college ever going to be paid for? What if they're not able to get a job? What then?

Our own thirteen kids, as you know by now, are all over the age map. So we're constantly dealing with things from all angles of childhood development. And since some of our children haven't belonged to us from birth, we also deal with broken places in their hearts and lives that are doubly hard to figure out as a parent, because we may not know—and certainly *they* don't know—exactly where the pain or emotion could be coming from. But one of the ways we try managing the impossibilities of all these spinning parts is by praying every day, "Lord, help me be aware *today* of each of my kids' needs."

Sometimes we can tell—the minute they walk in the door—one of them is going to need some cuddle time tonight. One of them may need us to look through their homework packet, helping to explain a concept or being sure they know what's expected of them for staying on task. One may need a tough-love moment. (We've got a good set of mom-eyes for that.) Another may need instead just a lot of grace and encouragement.

But whatever it is, we don't want to miss it—their specific need for today. Not just the general, boiler-plate stuff. The stock delivery of parenting goods. No, we're talking about the cry of their heart that we're likely to miss altogether if we're not locked in and looking for it. The *One* thing. The *now* thing. The *today* thing.

Because if you can get *those* right at a successful enough rate, then the scarier parts that are coming up later will just become the orderly ingredients of *another* day—a coming day when, like always (just like this morning), you wake up asking God to help you stay open, alert, and ready for the kinds of conversations and interactions that your kids are most in need of. So even when one of those fearful-sounding days comes barreling into the house one afternoon a few years from now, you'll be way more than ready for it. Prayed up for it. You'll have been establishing heart-to-heart trust and authenticity all along, steadily preparing for it—so that tomorrow's boy-friend trouble is as manageable at that point as the playground problems of fifteen years ago.

Because everything, at its root, is a *today* issue. Another Love One opportunity. And when you come to the ones in the future that seem most impossible, you might be shocked to see how capable a parent God's caused you to become. Without your really noticing.

That's the beauty of *One*.

So paste this principle onto whatever hairy challenge you're facing over the coming weeks and months. Bring it into the jury room where you're feeling condemned by guilt over your past sins, or feeling outpaced by people who make your life appear so dull and unfulfilling by contrast. Your path going forward is not a futile case of certain failure, and trying to escape or ignore its demands won't do anything but make it worse.

Start off today, tonight, or first thing in the morning with a new, open position of prayerfulness ("Whatever You say, Lord"), looking ahead with a willing spirit. With a faith-infused sense of watchfulness. And we guarantee you, God will put the impossible out to pasture.

You'll see.

Gotta Love It

Sitting here writing today, it's hard for us to describe our excitement level for you (and for us), realizing what all we stand to experience with God by embracing this everyday concept. One after another, He opens up ways for your faith to operate. He displaces your complacency. He instills in you an eternal perspective that starts to permeate the thinking behind your daily, weekly schedule. And before long, you're . . . oh, pick one:

You're helping a group of moms fill backpacks with school supplies and gift certificates for underprivileged students in your county.

You're becoming a host family for one of the kids from a nearby children's home, offering every-so-often getaways for a boy or girl who's dying for this kind of love and attention and long-term relationship.

You're taking your art skills downtown two nights a month to a homeless shelter, helping moms and their children create handmade pieces they can be proud of, building their self-esteem while breaking down your own misperceptions about who they are and what they need.

You're working together as a family to collect your spare change every month, earmarking it for missions or for sacks of groceries to donate to a food bank—anything besides casually blowing it on hot fudge sundaes at McDonalds, just because the money's lying around.

The possibilities are endless.

We can testify, in fact, from our current role at 147, that we're all the time being approached by people who want to meet for lunch, meet for coffee, get together to talk about questions they're having, to hear what we've learned that might be helpful to them and their families. We're honored to be asked, of course. We hope they'll always keep asking. But with everything we're currently juggling at home, we can't make ourselves completely round-the-clock available for every request. Simply can't be done. Wouldn't be good for anybody.

But instead of telling them to take a number, we've seen God bring a whole team of folks into our lives—women who've had specific experiences we know about—that we're often able to pair up with people to begin their own helpful dialogue. So today, if someone comes to us needing a friend to talk to, we might say, "You know what? We know a person who could really speak to what you're asking. Here's her name. Here's her number. Give her a call, and let us know how it goes." Not only does this spread out the work among additional helpers (which is one of those impossibility busters we talked about in chapter 6), but it also provides more people an opportunity for getting involved in hands-on, Love One encounters that otherwise they might never discover—ways for turning their knowledge, background, and wisdom into an all-around benefit for others.

And what works in our particular ministry, the same thing goes for all kinds of outreaches at your church or in your community—places where you could volunteer from your skill set and life story, becoming a mentoring figure for people you don't even know today, but who could be springs of new relationships tomorrow.

Don't knock it. Go try it.

Looking at your life this way is like taking one twist of a kaleidoscope, and suddenly you can see yourself becoming a picture of beauty and blessing in places that once seemed unimaginably too hard or too far out of reach for you. Learning to Love One just comes with so many great stories to tell.

Love stories like these . . .

(Suzanne) "Any professional would've told you," the doctor said—"in fact, *I* would've told you: this child (talking about JosieLove) needs significant attention. She needs to be

with parents who can focus all their energies on her alone."
That was the prevailing wisdom, the standard protocol, for
acclimating someone like Josie into a new environment, for
accelerating her progress toward maximum health.

One problem.

That's not the kind of home we had.

But instead, ours was the very kind of home she needed—
because within four or five weeks of being here with us, this
little three-and-a-half-year-old who'd never spoken much
more than a weakened, pitiful groan was already learning
and forming words and calling us all by name. This little girl
who could barely even stand, and could only transport herself
from place to place by crawling on all fours, was up and walking around and getting herself into mischief.

Why? How?

It's because she didn't have just a mom and dad to lavish
love and affection on her; she had six brothers and sisters who
smothered her with love in every room of the house. Love,
love, all the time love—smiling at her, patting on her, picking her up, playing with her. Stimulating her legs and joints,
squealing her name in gleeful excitement, gathering her into
the big circle of family, and never giving her a second when
she wasn't being adored and cared for.

What a sight. What a joy.

Our worst fears, at the moment of first discovery about
her condition, were that she'd never be able to function in
normal society. She might, we thought, even be a danger to
our other children and family. But after learning more, after
getting her meds put together—and most important, after
swamping her reservoir with more love than one little heart
and body could barely hold—she was percolating at high-
functioning capacity.

She went to day care. Did great. Went to preschool. Did
great. Started putting on weight. Growing. And today—what
a rascal—so smart, so cunning, oozing love onto everyone she

sees, becoming a hit with all her friends and schoolteachers. Her name, more than I could've even imagined, fits her like a glove.

"What we've seen here," the doctor said, "is that having your six other kids all around her, picking her up, knocking her down, was probably the best thing that could've happened to her. Medically, we wouldn't think she'd get what she needed in that environment. But in fact, she got more."

Because love can heal a lot of things.

(Gwen) We had a somewhat similar experience with our deaf child Joseph, who I worried from the outset would cause my mama heart to skip right out of my body for fear he wouldn't be able to keep up or would get lost, "Home Alone" style, in the mad-dash chaos of our family. He'd rarely been outside the walls of an African children's home, didn't know how to follow directions all that well. I was always cognizant of how easily he could wander himself into trouble without even realizing it. Keeping him out of danger became an overwhelming opponent in my head: "How do I get six kids out of the house, drag them all around to places, and not get him run over or left behind?"

Answer: "Jeremiah, you've got Joseph."

One of the best decisions I ever made had been taking our son Jeremiah—twelve years old at the time—to Uganda when we brought home Joseph and Daisy. He latched on to that experience with so much energy and enthusiasm, and God used it to ignite in him a genuine passion for third-world countries, serving the needy, and thinking outside the box in seeking to care for those less fortunate. I love seeing this Christ-like quality in him.

He and Joseph, in particular, really bonded during that time. And their brotherly connection has remained vividly strong in all the years since. So whenever we're out together, I don't worry too much about Joseph anymore, because Jeremiah's job—which he does so well—is to be sure Joseph is in the car, keeping up, being watched after. It's a sweet (I can still get away with calling my high school boy "sweet," can't I?)—a sweet expression of love that warms me to the core.

In fact—follow along with me here, just to get the full effect of it, and to see how God works in *any* of our lives when we focus on being a Love One kind of person. Jeremiah goes with us to Africa, truly gives of himself in caring for his new little brother. Beautiful. We get back to America, and their relationship continues to develop. Jeremiah, along with all our other kids, takes an interest in learning sign language so he can communicate with Joseph—another example of love in action. Then the next thing you know, he's coming home and telling me about a new cafeteria worker at school . . . who's deaf.

Think back with me now to your teenager days. Think of the menial laborers who worked at your school. Imagine one who's not able to hear or who possesses some other kind of noticeable difficulty. The other kids, the show-outs, make fun of him. Most at least just ignore him. Best case, you'll maybe smile at him when you pass by, try to be nice, but you'll think of him in sort of a condescending way, almost like how you'd pat a dog from the neighborhood that routinely showed up on campus.

And yet here's Jeremiah, not just acting friendly toward this cafeteria helper, but genuinely excited about being able to sign with him everyday. He's thinking ahead of time about what he wants to be sure to tell him. They've hit it off so well, in fact, this guy has started coming to some of Jeremiah's basketball games. My son's got a new fan, as well as a new friend . . . all because he's operating out of a mind-set of love.

See how fluid and natural this is? We make a commitment, like Jeremiah did, to love someone, the way he opened up his heart to love Joseph despite his hearing impairment. The next thing you know, your relationship with that person is growing and deepening, rich with God's blessing. Then the Lord, picking up on what He's been teaching you and developing in you through *One* interaction, leads you to another that He's opened your eyes to recognize. And then instead of being an "Oh, great. *Really?* Do I *have* to do that?"—as if He's twisting your arm—it's like the most exciting, refreshing, energizing experience you can think of. You can't believe God allows you to do something so helpful to others without it feeling like a drudgery and sacrifice. That's not to say it can't be costly—to your time, to your schedule, maybe even to your reputation—but the joy always outweighs the expense, by a mile. God is using you to do His work. People are receiving from you His grace and goodness.

Who can't see the surpassing value in that?

(Us) So don't think we're trying to drag you kicking and screaming into a lifestyle that represents your own worst nightmare. Loving the one in front of you, doing the next thing the Lord asks of you, making the commitment *today* that you will serve others out of a simple, surrendered heart of worship—we're talking about the *good life* here.

It's like cool water on your thirsty soul.

We introduced you in the last chapter to our friend John, who does the sewing on our bags and other items. We wish you could be here to meet him. He is such a contagiously joyful kind of guy. His smile is so full and bright. Just lights up the room and makes you feel good, simply by being around him.

As we were preparing for one of our recent trips to Africa, the Lord gave us the idea of taking John along as well. His mother had died in Sudan during the previous year, and he obviously hadn't been able to see her or spend time with her before she passed away. The effervescent smile he emits without even trying—we'd noticed it had seemed a little distant and more difficult for him to work up in the past six to eight months. He was sad.

So we pitched the idea to him of going to Africa with us, and he readily accepted. He could hardly believe it, in fact. So off we went. And while we two ladies were working in Uganda for a couple of weeks, we put John on a little puddle jumper and sent him off to Sudan to reconnect with his people and his village. Gave him a little prepaid phone so he could stay in contact with us, and we heard from him nearly every day. So excited.

But times are hard there. It is, after all, an impoverished, imploded, basically impossible place to live. And when we got back home, and he filled us in on some of the things he'd seen while visiting, we could tell his heart was still broken.

A guy like John, you might think, after returning to the States, would just flow back seamlessly into his nice, busy life, relieved to be down the street again from an abundantly stocked grocery store. Because, yeah, he's got it good. Got it made. And since he can't really do anything to fix what's so wrong in a place like Sudan . . . life just needs to go on. They'll just need to keep going on too.

And yet John came home with a lingering burden for his village. Many were sick. HIV-positive. Full-blown AIDS. Lots of them were dying. And most fundamental of all, they had no real access to clean water. The nearest reliable source required a two-and-a-half hour, back-breaking walk to get there. Hardly a livable, sustainable solution.

The Lord, as we've mentioned, had been leading us already to begin doing some well-digging projects, providing water for some of the areas we seek to serve. Fresh water is such a natural extension of our heartbeat at 147. I mean, what good is medical care or school buildings or feeding programs if people can't even be assured of getting clean water every day?

But Sudan. How could we do it? The companies we contacted for help and information said, "There's so much bedrock in that area, it's hard to tell if we can successfully drill there." Even being able to pinpoint John's village on the map was no easy task in trying to determine the viability of such an endeavor. In the end, it took us a full year to locate a partner and put together all the logistics. The weather worked against us. Delays became the norm. It wasn't easy. Seemed darn near impossible at times. But the Lord kept working, of course, and so did we. And today, John's people and family, along with all the people of his Sudanese village, enjoy water at the ready, right there within sight of their dwellings.

All because John was committed to Love One. And because we and our families were committed to Love One. And because the people who gave money to support the project were also committed to Love One. And more than anything, we think, simply this:

Because God just loves it when His children . . .

Love One.

One and Only

End of the day, that's all we wanted this book to be about. *Love One.*

We've always used those words as one of our logos. It's a concept we've tried to live by and be led by. Not in a Peace Corps kind of way, but purely in a surrendered response to the Lord, a grateful reaction to His saving grace, a desire to be His hands and feet on the earth, bringing glory to His great name and operating as His willing servants.

Not every day do we hit it out of the park. Some days we go down swinging. And some days, to be quite honest with you, we don't even feel like going up to bat. But we do keep trying—as we hope you're trying, and will always keep trying—to put ourselves on the back burner in all-day surrender to God.

"What's the next thing, Lord?"

Do that.
"And then the next thing?"
Do that.
That *One* thing.
And before you know it, you're doing the impossible.

Epilogue

Impossible Keeps Coming

THANK YOU.

What an incredible blessing to know you're still here, still reading, all the way to the end. If our prayers for you are reaching anywhere near their full effect, you're hopefully feeling very encouraged and excited right now, hyped up on what your life can become by saying yes to God—always yes to God—each day, at each opportunity. The power of a single "yes," piled one on top of the other, can take you to places you never dreamed possible. And the more often you say it, no matter how difficult or challenging or against your grain, the next one will bubble up from inside you with greater ease, until one day you'll hear it simply jumping off your lips, lickety-split. Before you're even able to rein it back in, it's already out there, pulling you along in the direction of total openness and obedience. "Wait, *what* did I just say?"

You said yes.

And in God's hands, it's making all the difference.

So we *cannot wait* to hear from you about all the things God has done and will do through your life as you go all-in with Him. It is truly the only way to fly.

But what we *don't* want you to take away from this experience we've shared together is the idea that every time you respond in agreement with what God is leading you to do, the early returns will always come back an immediate success. Not every journey of "fun, blind faith" is certain to end up wrapped in gift paper with a pretty bow tied across the lid. Happy endings are not the goal; the prize is the joy of knowing that what you're doing, you're doing for Jesus. That's all the reason and reward you need.

We also hope, in addition, we've shattered the notion that being a Love One person is sort of like Navy Seal training, where you go through this rigorous program of discipline, challenge, and surrender for a period of years, and then finally you come out wearing the uniform—an official, recognized, spiritual warrior, with the certified gold pin blazing on your chest. You've made it. You're a pro. No. This adventure with God we're talking about doesn't suddenly plateau and level out, and then the rest of your life is like being a superhero. Saying "yes" becomes easier—yes, it does—but what it means in real time will always be a wall-climbing exercise of harrowing faith.

That's why we often remind ourselves and others that our goal, at the end of our days, is not to *run* into the arms of Jesus, but to *crawl* there—blisters on our hands, sweat dripping from our chins, our pants legs worn through at the knees, with just enough energy left to fall at His feet. Exhausted. *[Whump.]* Believers who want to sashay into heaven with their hair all in place and their jacket pressed and dry cleaned, looking the part of a Christian superstar— oh, the blessings they've missed. What do they think was the whole point of this? From how we read the Bible, every day on Earth is meant to be a grateful, deliberate opportunity to be

Christ's servant, to become the living extension of His hands and feet on Earth. And when one of those days becomes our *last* day, we want to be sure we've spent every ounce of energy doing exactly that. Nothing left on the field. Nothing held in reserve. Blood and tears and burning hot muscles.

And we'll rest when we get there.

We'll rest when we're with Him.

So be sure those two things are clear, that you're not hearing us trying to sell you on a life that's peaches and cream and always suitable for framing. Saying yes to Him, living the *One* lifestyle, is—no doubt—so invigorating, so full, so satisfying. Puts a smile on our face just thinking about it. Wouldn't trade it for anything in the world. And yet it can often look messy. And it never gets easy. And that's okay.

It's all for You, Jesus.

Because what good is a life that says anything else?

In fact, just in the relatively brief time since we first sat down to start discussing and then writing this book, we've continued to see God stretching us and growing us beyond where He'd even taken us before. Perfect world, we thought His Spirit could maybe have held off on the next set of "opportunities" for a little while until we'd sort of finished up on this one. Would've felt a little cleaner, seems like. But what kind of book can you really write on obedience and surrender if you're hoping He'll basically leave you alone so you can get your work done? If what we're talking about is truly supposed to make any sense, then we can't ever be going around feeling like, "Yeah, we got this." Instead, we must always be trusting, always leaning in, always confident He knows our limits a lot better than we do.

(Gwen) So one day I'm driving around with a friend, Kelly, who runs a local ministry. Her job that afternoon was to help an eighteen-year-old junior get enrolled in a new high school, since his mom had recently moved out of town and left her son, unimaginably, behind.

I'm up in the front seat, where Kelly's driving, and Kevin—the teenage kid—is in the back. I'd never met him in my life before ten minutes ago, when he first crawled in. And yet as clear as day, that sense of Holy Spirit rumbling started working its way up through my body and into my head, causing this one thought to begin pulsing with that familiar, God-inspired echo: "He's at a crossroads, Gwen. He's either going *this* way, or he's going *that* way."

I'd like to play dumb here. Act like I really wrestled and debated for days with what I was thinking. But I knew what I was supposed to do. I knew what "yes" meant in that situation—not because every opportunity to help and serve is automatically mine to do, but because I've lived with God in this trusting relationship long enough that I can much more easily tell now when He's handing something off to *me.*

So after talking it over with Scott, we—yeah, we brought Kevin home to live with us. He stayed for about six months. He ate at our table, he flowed into our schedule. We didn't know where it was going or what form it would ultimately take, but we just knew we were being faithful to the Lord in offering him a bed and a family to belong to.

And at first, he really seemed to take to it. He'd rarely if ever known a life that contained any structure and continuity. So he liked knowing that his needs were being cared for. He appreciated the support. We told him he was welcome to stay, that we'd help him look into college, that we'd be his home, and that we'd be here for him all the way.

But then he . . . he decided this wasn't what he wanted. And he left.

Not long afterward, a similar thing occurred, only this time the one who was bringing someone home to stay with us was Scott, not me. Through a situation he'd encountered at work, he met Jonathan, a twenty-four-year-old man with a number of troubling, special needs. His father had moved away, leaving no one to care for this young man who, obviously, was not totally able to manage himself independently. And Scott had come home feeling as though we should see what we could do about it ourselves.

I remember, as we were discussing it, we decided to bring our older son into the room, to let him know what we were considering, see what he thought. We talked about the different kinds of attention a young man like this would require, and how including him as part of our family, for whatever length of time, would force some adjustments to our usual flow. It might be really crazy, we admitted. We might be taking on something we have no business trying to handle, we said. But I'll never forget Jeremiah saying, with somewhere close to half a shrug, "Isn't that just what we do, Mom?"

Yeah. I guess it is.

But after six weeks, and after deliberations with a family counselor from church, we realized Jonathan's needs were more severe than we were equipped to handle. With help, we found a living situation for him that could do a more complete job of assisting him.

And like Kevin—just like that—he was gone.

People might think, "Well, I guess you didn't hear God right on that one, huh?" Uh, yeah, I think we did. We still get texts and Facebook messages from Kevin (and his mail!) fairly routinely. He says to tell the kids hello. We tell him we're always praying for him, that we love him and care for him. We don't know yet what might eventually come of all this.

And Scott also still checks in on Jonathan. We buy his groceries every week. We give him rides to the doctor, trying to do whatever we can do to help him. We don't know what it all might mean. Not yet. Too soon to tell.

But here's the thing: There was a point in my life when I would *never* have put myself in the car with someone like Kelly, out on a rescue run for her ministry. There was a point in my life when I would *never* have considered—not for a single, split second—the idea of putting a Kevin or a Jonathan into my crazy-filled life with six kids, swapping rooms, and adding more laundry.

And yet because of what started—not that many years ago—with a simple yes of surrender to God, He has opened up our lives to amazing adventures that, even in not turning into Hallmark movies every time, turn us every day into people who are a lot more joyful and exciting to live with. What matters is not what it ends up looking like; what matters is what we end up being like. And where those planted seeds end up sprouting in the years to come—that's God's business to figure out, not ours.

(Suzanne) But then on the other hand, our last year or two has been one of those seasons when God decided to go ahead and just show us, right up front, the fruit of our obedience. He obviously can do it either way, or do it both ways at the same time. Our job is just to say yes, and then let Him do the driving.

We met a young woman named Anne Marie while on one of our family's trips to Honduras, where she was working with us as a translator. She was a beautiful girl, so sweet, but very quiet and introverted. Kind of a perplexing combination of signals—enough that you could tell, there was a story underneath.

And the more we found out, the more we felt ourselves drawn to her. She was actually one of the kids who'd lived in the Coppromé children's home, had left at eighteen with two plastic grocery bags of belongings, and had moved in with friends to try making it somewhat on her own. She wanted to go to college but didn't actually even know where her next meal was coming from. So even with all her promise, she had little to no opportunity.

Unless . . .

She actually became, for us, the spark that lit our Madrina program in Honduras—the transition homes we talked about in chapter 7, which Raul is now so instrumental in overseeing.

Anne Marie was the first. And before we'd even left Honduras on that one trip when we met her, we each felt the Holy Spirit leading us to tell her, "You're one of ours now, if you want to be. You're part of our family. We will be here for you, we will help you, and we will give you what you need so you can dream big and become everything God desires for you."

A day later—literally—we noticed she'd already changed the profiles on all her social media to read: Anne Marie Mayernick. Not that we'd officially adopted her or anything. She's too old for that. And yet she had already become, both in *her* heart as well as ours, a full-fledged member of our yes-breathing family.

I guess, even after being around so many places now where children are abandoned and unwanted, even after adopting three kids into our own family and working with hundreds of others who are doing the same, the shock of seeing just how desperately a person can crave to belong never quite ceases to amaze. Everything that made this one young girl appear somewhat sullen and distant to us at first came almost entirely from not having anyone to believe in her, nobody to love on her, no place to truly call home.

But now, she's enrolled in a private university there in Honduras, majoring in international relations, hoping to someday work in the U.S. embassy or in some kind of nonprofit. She's living in a stable home environment, supported by the incredible people who care and give to 147. She holds her head up high and hangs with a group of good, loving friends. She plays soccer. She's on a dance team. She's bloomed into a beautiful little flower who's caring for herself as a thriving adult.

And she's a Mayernick, same as all the rest of my kids.

And I don't know any way to tell you how impossible this scenario would've seemed to me, even five years ago, maybe less. This is not something Suzanne ever saw herself doing, any more than Gwen did—I assure you of that.

Yet look—here I am.

Look—here we are.

And don't look now—but the next *One* is you.

See You Around

(Us) We thought writing this book would be impossible.

It wasn't.

Of course.

But that's not to say the next thing that comes along won't feel even more daunting. In fact, we're pretty sure it will.

And one of the ways that God is going to pump us full of joy as we keep living out each new impossibility will come from knowing that someone like you is out there doing the same thing, pushing the edges, daring to follow. Then, like us, you'll look back amazed at how far He's brought you, until you won't quite be able to even remember or recognize that person who used to be so afraid, so resistant, so full of excuses . . . and so empty of joy.

How thankful we are to God for making a life this thrilling available to people like us, and yet never making it any harder to attain and receive than by simply loving the *One* person in front of us, doing the *One* next thing He's telling us, and believing in the only *One* whose glory shines through it—and through us—from beginning to end.

The impossible really does start right there.

ACKNOWLEDGMENTS

From Suzanne

Mike—Without you this journey would have never begun. Thanks for allowing me to follow God's gentle whisper in my ears. I love you.

Grace, Michael, Annabelle, MillerAnne, Joshua, JosieLove, Caleb—Your lives are what wrote the words of this book in my heart. Thank you for inspiring me to love others more. MaMa loves you!

Poppie, Nonnie, Pop, and Gran—Thanks for the countless hours you have spent serving us. It could not have been done without you! I love you!

Tara—my sister, my friend. Always "on call," my safe place, my dependable place of comfort, my place of peace. Not sure what I would do without you. You are truly an angel in my life. Thank you.

Gwen—my partner in crime. Who else would walk with me on this crazy bold journey of faith? God knew EXACTLY what He was doing. I am so blessed and thankful to have you alongside me each and every day! I love you, sister!

From Gwen

Scott—You are my "Always and Forever." Thanks for encouraging me to spread my wings and chase God's calling. Your leading allowed me to follow the Lord's voice. I love you!

Jeremiah "My Heart," Elijah "My Joy," Emily "My Light," Maggie "My Hope," Joseph "My Strength," Daisy "My Grace"—You have taught me more about Jesus than any other experience in my life. I am humbled to be your mom, and I am so thankful God has our family on this amazing adventure together. I love ya TONS!

Retta, BooBoo, Nana—Thanks for all the extra hands and love. The way you love my babies and serve Scott and me is a true blessing. Love you!

Mom and Dad—Your encouragement is a priceless gift. Thanks for always being in my corner. Love you!

Denise Long and Laura Moritz—You opened up my mind, heart, and hands so that I could speak to my angel Joseph.

Emily Chapman Richards—Thanks for sharing your heart and challenging us to listen to God's voice.

Suzanne—I couldn't imagine this journey with anyone else. You see the real, raw me, and you still love me. Scripture says that there is a friend who sticks closer than a brother, and you are MY PERSON. I love you with my whole heart. Thanks for always having my back. Love ya, sister!